ARE YOU LUCKY?

*Our attempts to influence fate—and
dealing with what we get.*

All inquiries should be addressed to:

Book Domain LLC.
543 E Louise Dr Phoenix, Az 85050

Ordering Information:
Amount Deals. Special rebates are accessible on the amount bought by corporations, associations, and others. For points of interest, contact the distributor at the address above.

Printed in the United States of America.

ISBN-13   Paperback   978-1-964100-30-2
            eBook   978-1-964100-31-9

Library of Congress Control Number: 2024925492

ARE YOU
LUCKY?

Our attempts to influence fate—
and dealing with what we get.

BRIAN HALE

BOOK DOMAIN LLC
Publish to Perfection

MY SINCERE THANKS...

I owe a debt of gratitude to many people for their encouragement and conversations, which caused this book to evolve from an idea to a reality. While there are many thanks due to people who contributed in small ways to this effort, here are some people who were pivotal in helping bring this book to life.

Burma Kroger
Dave Temple
Nancy Becker
Pamela Hale—for being my far-better half!
Zachary Baehr
Chad Wilken, for being willing to tackle my technology needs.

And all the soldiers mentioned herein,
who fought overseas so I could live and write freely.

For more discussion about luck, and its role in our lives, please go to our website: www.areyouluckybook.com

CONTENTS

CHAPTER 1: How Luck is Woven Into Our Lives.................................... 1

CHAPTER 2: Luck At the Tip of the Chainsaw 13

CHAPTER 3: Where Did Luck Come From in Our Language? 27

CHAPTER 4: What Is Luck?.. 35

CHAPTER 5: Luck from the Heavens Above.. 39

    God's Role in Our Fortunes.. 40

    Being Fortunate... 54

CHAPTER 6: Physical Forces Impacting Our Luck 67

    Astrology and Its Role in Our Fates... 73

    Superstitions 82

    "Weather" We Are Lucky or Not 96

    Is There Something in a Number?.. 106

CHAPTER 7: Luck As a Life Response... 115

    On the Nature of Luck, by Roy Posner....................................... 117

    Taking Responsibility for Our Own Luck 130

    How's Your Karma?.. 136

CHAPTER 8: Dumb Luck.. 145

CHAPTER 9: The Lucky Forces Inside of Us 153

    Trusting Your Instincts.. 154

    The Voice... 160

    Luck's Dark Side 166

    Working "In the Zone" 172

CHAPTER 10: The Lucky Forces Outside of Us 185

    Our Luck in Games of Chance 186

    Lucky In War? 200

    Lucky in Love? 217

CHAPTER 11: Now That We've Found Luck, What Are We Going

    to Do With It? 229

    "So, What Do You Know?" About The Author 247

CHAPTER 1

How Luck Is Woven Into Our Lives

Luck is everything... My good luck in life was to be a really frightened person. I'm fortunate to be a coward, to have a low threshold of fear, because a hero couldn't make a good suspense film.

— Alfred Hitchcock

So much of our lives are spent adjusting to the trials and tribulations that befall us. As we plunge headlong into this world, we change everything we touch. Every outcome in the world is subject to change, based on the presence (or absence) of each of us.

At some point, though, each of us has endured a challenging spot in our lives that leaves us wondering, "How did *that* happen the way it did?"

The number of possible outcomes is so great in most situations that it is impossible for our modest minds to calculate the possibilities. Unable to fully explain many given outcomes logically, the most expedient alternative is to blame luck. Luck is promoted as an invisible, omnipresent force credited with the ability to alter every outcome. If it really does exist as a physical force of the universe, though, why are there so many varying versions of its work among the cultures of the world? How can some cultures and belief systems dismiss it completely?

Through the course of life, we all run into people who just seem to be luckier than the rest of us. These are the people whose toast must always hit the floor peanut-butter-side-up. Each of us could probably name a person who seems to have very few redeeming qualities, yet seems to always land on his or her feet when faced with adversity. We also know people who live under the dark cloud of misfortune. If something bad could happen, it will likely happen to them.

So, if we are all created equal, how do the lucky and the unlucky develop side-by-side within the same basic culture? Where does luck come from? How do we decide, in a complex set of daily developments, whether we were fortunate or very unfortunate? How much of every outcome hinges on the perspective we bring to the situation, and the lessons we take away?

Life is full of ups and downs. Every day, the winds of fate toss us from one side of our personal lifeboat to the other. On any given day:

- There was a great song on the radio when my alarm went off this morning.

- The coffee maker went on the fritz at breakfast.
- My shoestring broke while getting ready for work.
- Today's the day I get to wear my lucky tie.
- Make a sack lunch, or go to a local restaurant? Flip a coin.
- The paper boy actually got the newspaper onto the porch!
- The sun is reaching far enough north to melt the frost from my windshield. No scraping today!
- Nearly every traffic light came up green on the way to work.
- My favorite parking space at work is occupied.
- I toss a penny into the fountain at lunch.
- The server is down at work, meaning everyone is going "cold turkey" on the computer for awhile. Good for me, bad for my co-worker who is on a deadline.
- Unable to "compute," employees take the opportunity to push away from the work station and talk face-to-face with their co-workers, and actually get to appreciate people inside the position.
- During those discussions, another co-worker discloses he has tickets he cannot use to the big game this weekend. Now my wife and I will be going.
- On the way home, I find a gas station just dropping the price-per-gallon, so I decide to fill up the gas tank and buy a Powerball ticket.

Every one of these occurrences gives us the opportunity to assign the direction of our fates. While there are the day-to-day victories and annoyances to keep track of, as we age, we are better equipped to step back and take a big-picture view of the events in our lives, and possibly even alter our views about the impact of each event.

Over the course of any given day, it is quite surprising how many times people bow in the direction of luck. As we hear about a big event coming up in a friend's life, almost without thinking about it, we will wish them good luck in their endeavors. We may not always know exactly what good luck will look like in their situation, but we wish it for them all the same.

Conversely, it is a common saying that bad things happen in threes. I have heard this applied to celebrity deaths and mechanical break-downs around the house. Not that individuals among the pool of celebrities ever stop dying, or that appliances ever stop wearing out, but the saying still applies to groupings of these unfortunate events—perhaps as a way to help us mentally limit our losses. Perhaps the saying became popular because we want to create a limit to the amount of bad news we have to digest at once.

Luck is a tricky concept because it can change its appearance without changing its face. In the heat of the moment, it might have been easy to believe a chance meeting with that woman (or man) at the bar was the luckiest moment of your life. But quite often—and sometimes sooner rather than later—you come to see how that encounter was the *worst* thing that could have happened to you.

Sometimes we simply want to believe the script we are writing for our lives is going to work out just the way we want it to. And we want to believe it in the worst way. So we do.

Our first-blush reaction to any situation is much like our long-term view, in that it will vary based on whether we approach the situation with pessimism, optimism, or realism.

The concept of luck in our lives can become a deeply philosophical consideration. Two people involved in the same natural disaster can come away feeling they experienced a tremendous amount of good luck or an unfathomable amount of bad luck. Maybe the perspective is based on whether they place more value on all the family heirlooms and the full sets of baseball cards saved since childhood—or their lives.

What's more, those assessments of "good" and "bad" can also be revised after a few months have passed, and for a variety of reasons.

Because, as mere humans, we cannot immediately identify the origins of the things (good and bad) happening to us in a given day, we find it easier—given our perception of the linear facts of the situation—to quickly assign the credit or blame on the doorstep of luck. But blaming luck is most often a simple and incomplete solution for a complex set of causes-and-effects, which cause our lives to turn out the way they do.

"This was my lucky day!" or "I couldn't catch a break today!" Which story you will use to describe your experience depends almost exclusively on you, and your reaction to what happens in front of you. At its core, it appears each person's classification of luck comes down to whether they focus on what they have lost, what they have gained, or what they might have avoided.

"What you focus on will expand," has become a mantra on the corporate motivational speaker circuit. I think that is generally true. Because your life is uniquely yours, you are the only one who must endure ALL of your ups and downs. Even if you are confined to a hospital bed, the nurses will change shifts. You will still be with you.

Still, our lives (and the outcomes which we produce) are the result of many different influences. The days of our lives are littered with quantum (layered) influences, both mechanical and human. Many of these influences are beyond our control. The only thing within our grasp to control, most of the time, is our reaction to the particular situation.

This interrelationship leaves us as the sole keepers of the power to set the tone for our day. Others *can* do it for you, but you have to cede them the authority. Focus on the positives (no matter how small currently), and they will grow. Ignore the negatives (to the extent you can) and they will cease to hold such an important place in your brain. This is, of course, easier said at a podium for $5,000 per hour than it is done in our personal lives.

The quest of this book is to shine a light on the dark corners of our consciousness where we conjure up our luck. We will explore the origins of luck and how it has woven its way into every culture on Earth. Up front, let me say I have no deep understanding of the cosmos, and therefore I cannot dismiss the validity of any particular brand of luck. I personally believe there is merit in some areas, and I believe people are just kidding themselves in others. But I *do not know* with any kind of absolute certainty what kinds of luck have merit, and which do not. I must admit that I adhere to some lucky rituals, not because I know they work, but because I can't be sure they don't. Since it's not much trouble to cover some of fate's bases, I knock on wood once in a while. And I go to church occasionally.

From the first successful hunting experience by our ancestors living in caves, humans have been adopting rituals they believe will replicate a similarly successful experience next time. Some of those rituals truly contribute to the potential for success, while others are designed to create more of a mental advantage than a physical one. The primary benefit of some rituals is to simply intimidate the competition into thinking you have the forces of luck working in your favor. Or maybe it is just a mechanism you use to convince yourself.

Early in life, each of us is exposed to the magic of luck. From the early days of walking to school I remember being told, "Step on a crack, break your mother's back." Who thought up that crazy cause-and-effect relationship?

As we grew up, many of us sent out pleas for the Gods of luck to smile upon us during tests in school. There became, and still exists, many theories about how to pull the right multiple-choice answer out of thin air when God isn't speaking loud enough for us to hear. Making sure you are sitting next to the smarter girls in class is never bad luck in that regard, although the smart girls tend to be less accommodating in letting you see their papers.

Once out of school, there are also many opportunities for our lives to change based on a chance. Because you decide to pursue one path or the other, your life can be changed forever. The same will be true tomorrow, when you come upon another fork in the road. There is also a regular stream of weather phenomena, fast cars, weapons, power tools, and diseases that can change the course of our lives in an instant.

The extent to which we are lucky enough to avoid all of the potholes lying before us is the extent to which we can move forward in performing the flimsy life script we are writing for ourselves. However, when (not "if") a serious detour comes before us, and the script changes radically, there may come a time when we will feel lucky to still be performing from any script at all.

There are so many life choices littered throughout each of our days. We can understand the wisdom of not breaking mirrors or walking under ladders. The potential for injury is obvious in these situations. But crossing a black cat's path? Or starting a new project on a Friday? Or waiting until the moon is no longer full to undertake a task?

Humans have been deciding things for years by flipping a coin. Some people have, when faced with two basically even choices, flipped a coin and never looked at the final position of the coin, moving ahead with the option their intuition really wanted. At some point in the preparation, or the flip (according to this line of thinking), your mind chooses a side to "root" for and reveals your true desire. On the other hand, I always felt obliged to honor the science of the coin, and do what I pledged to do if it came up heads. Or I'd go two-out-of-three (or five-out-of-nine).

Where does all of this tomfoolery come from, and should we let it dictate our life's decisions? Can we manipulate the various systems at play to make sure we get as much, or more, of the luck we deserve? Or perhaps this is all just an elaborate method we humans have devised to describe the sordid story of our lives.

"As luck would have it," is a superficial way of glossing over all of the things you may, or may not, have done to cause something to turn out the way it did. It also discounts all of the things other people may, or may not, have done to impact the outcome. What I have learned in my first half-century on Earth is that no one is a success or a failure in a vacuum. On a planet with seven billion people (and growing), it is difficult to accomplish anything without the contribution of some other human being. What's more, we all influence the events within our own personal sphere. If you touch something, you change it.

Given the pervasive nature of luck in our culture, I was surprised in my research to find the subject had not really been thoroughly discussed in book form. As I continued digging, I think I may have discovered why past authors have shied away from the subject. Luck is difficult to put a fence around, let alone define. In some quarters, it borders on witchcraft, and leads to an attempt to understand the allure of tarot cards. In others, it may be seen as an assault on your belief in God (or perhaps the *reason* for your belief in God).

Still, nobody has been able to quantify the physical property of luck. The concept is something that bounces around in each of our heads, but it is difficult to define on paper, or hold in our hands. It is less an object and more of a force. But is there any way to objectively measure this force to prove its existence? As such, might it be better described as a phenomenon?

So far, the din each of us creates to subjectively measure luck's impact in our lives drowns out anyone who wants to look at the subject rationally. In some ways, I understand how many of us may not *want* to know if an objective force of luck actually exists. The notion (and my experience) that luck can appear "out of nowhere" is inspiring to humans. It feeds the part of our brain that is determined to never give up. If we ever discover there are some rational properties of luck, and you can absolutely determine you aren't running into any this month, it would likely change your outlook and your effort.

Despite its uncertain nature, we all still grasp for the notion that luck is out there, and many of us regularly participate in its rituals.

If you ever wondered how luck rose to such a revered place in our society, given its rather shady existence, this will be a frolicking and enjoyable read. The quotes sprinkled throughout this book are presented to illustrate that luck has been called to answer for many of humankind's successes and failures. We will explore many real-life experiences described herein, some of them deeply personal. I also share these pages with an array of people with whom I have come into contact over the years, who have graciously shared their own stories as it relates to their fate. There are also public stories of people I wouldn't necessarily rate as friends, but certainly they are good people who have been in the public eye during the years I have been paying attention.

All of the people mentioned herein are merely regular people using the gifts they were born with to get through on the rocky road of life. Not unlike each of you.

I am hopeful this book will encourage you to explore your own pivotal life experiences (because everyone has them), and perhaps recognize where fate, fortune, karma, or just dumb luck came into play to make you the person you are today. My goal is to make this exercise instructive, and provide an informative platform from which to plan the next moves in our lives. Whether or not we are planning a "next move" in life, forces have already been set in motion to create one for us. One virus, one patch of ice, or one incoming antagonist is all that is needed to change the script of our lives.

I hope you are lucky in navigating those changes. In order for your luck to be as good as it can be, let's see if we can identify what luck really is, where you can look for it, and how you can harness it for your personal benefit.

I will begin by describing how luck has been most often assigned to me.

CHAPTER 2

LUCK AT THE TIP OF THE CHAINSAW

"The only good luck many great men ever had was being born with the ability and determination to overcome bad luck."

— Channing Pollock

My quest for the meaning of luck began many years ago in the mountains of Colorado. My dad learned many ways to be frugal, working as the sole breadwinner for a family of five kids and a stay-at-home wife. He worked in the assembly portion of a variety of major daily newspapers across America. Coupon-clipping became a weekly ritual at my house, and we were subsequently introduced to a number of excess coupons for newly crafted items in the 1970s, an era of food invention—Pringles, anyone?

One of the places we lived during my developing years was Lakewood, Colorado. Lakewood was—and still is—a good place to live in the western suburbs of Denver. Tucked up against the eastern slope of the Rocky Mountains, the area held many opportunities for a young lad and his dad to participate in some "male bonding" activities.

From paper routes to a wide variety of sporting events, I can appreciate (now) that I ran my parents a little ragged. Their raggedness had at least something to do with my four younger siblings, who often needed things at the same time—at least that's my egocentric view of the situation. What else are younger brothers and sisters for, but to provide a scapegoat for the oldest?

One day, as my dad drove home from his job at the Denver Post, he heard a radio report that the U.S. Forest Service had taken down a vast swath of pine trees in the mountains above Boulder, Colorado suffers from an almost never-ending cycle of pine beetle disease, which regularly thins out the trees that make the Rocky Mountains so beautiful.

In response, the Forest Service occasionally comes through and clears out strips of the beetle-infested forest to make it a healthier place for trees not yet afflicted. On this particular occasion, the forest rangers turned to the public to help clean up the forest floor in exchange for some free firewood.

One of the many tricks my father picked up along the frugality trail is the ability to heat your home with a wood-burning stove. At the newspaper, they always had a surplus of wooden pallets, which could be cut into stove-sized pieces and burned to save hundreds of dollars on a winter's heating bill. Since burning wood in the fireplace without restriction was still allowed in Denver in the 1970s (air pollution concerns have since put a crimp on the activity), the report of free wood always attracted his attention.

I don't know that this happened but I can certainly imagine my dad driving down the road only half-listening to the radio. I can see his head snapping to attention when the announcer got to the "FREE" part.

"Son," he said upon his arrival at home, "be ready when I get off work on Sunday morning. We are going to the mountains to get some firewood."

His work at the Denver Post required him to work long hours, particularly on the weekends. The Sunday paper always attracted a wide range of retailers trying to coax citizens into their stores to buy their products. Each Sunday, local daily papers all over the country come stuffed with advertising from every big name (and several small name) stores in any given town. My dad made a career out of stuffing those inserts into the paper. So on Saturday nights, he always worked into Sunday morning until the papers were sent out to the delivery trucks at about 3 a.m.

It was a Sunday morning ritual for Dad to come home after work, take a shower and have a bite to eat. Usually, he would try to steal a couple of hours of sleep before he got up to whisk his family off to church. But in the wee hours of this particular Sunday in early October, he knew his day was not over. He had gotten his friend, Jim DeVaney, interested in the concept of free wood, too. So before he went to meet Jim, he went downstairs to wake up his eldest son for a wood-cutting expedition.

I was seventeen years old on October 3, 1978. I was just settling into my senior year at Bear Creek High School. I played a little baseball, and worked irreverently as a columnist for the student newspaper on campus, *Bear Facts*. A year before, several friends joined me in producing an underground newspaper in the spirit of our Monty Python-soaked minds, *Barely Facts*. I was a smart-ass then, and many would say I never fully lost that trait. But the point is, I was a stereotypical high school student. Getting up at the crack of dawn wasn't something I did by choice.

My slovenly habits were no concern of my dad's that day. We were going to head into the mountains to get some FREE wood. I have always loved the Rocky Mountains, and in the morning, as the sun is coming up, it is truly heavenly. My dad and I never hunted together, but "hunting" firewood presented itself as an equivalent activity. And if it all went well, I would still get home in time to get a couple of hours of rest before the Denver Broncos football game later that afternoon.

Groaning in faint protest as I slid out of bed, I shimmied into my jeans and threw on a T-shirt, a flannel shirt and windbreaker. Jim was expecting to meet us at his house in thirty minutes, so I brushed my teeth, ran a comb through my hair, and within ten minutes, we were on our way.

It was still dark as we drove north toward Jim's house. Jim was one of the handiest men I have ever known. As far as I could tell, there is no tool ever created that he couldn't use effectively. He was a whiz with cars, and even garaged a couple of classic vehicles, so he could restore them in his spare time. Among his wide array of tools, he had a selection of chainsaws from which we could choose. We loaded our weapons of tree destruction, and followed Jim's full-sized pickup west toward Boulder. I was mostly just snoozing in the passenger seat as we rolled through the city of Boulder and up into Boulder Canyon.

Several hairpin turns on our way up the canyon rousted me back to consciousness. The sun was beginning to peak over the horizon, and long shadows began to form in the mountain canyons. Just off the paved highway, and off onto a couple of dirt roads, we came to a sign posted by the Forest Service. In the ravine below us lay several hundred large forest pine trees that we could see, strewn flat on the ground. They were in no particular order. Some were lying over the top of others, and stumps were everywhere.

Our task lay before us . . . literally.

So we pulled off the road, off the trail a little bit so others could get in, and got ready to start lumberjacking. We got the chainsaws out of the back of Jim's truck, and we all put our gloves on.

But how do you approach an 80-foot-tall pine tree? Neither my Dad nor I were rugged outdoorsmen. We've always done what we had to, but it usually was never done according to the book. That's not his fault, nor mine. Neither one of us was thoroughly trained. We made our way by improvising.

In this predicament, we decided a little teamwork was in order. Sawing a tree that is lying flat on the ground creates challenges. The weight of these trees is substantial, and lying flat on the ground, it is difficult to saw completely through. We decided that I would get one end of the tree up on a stump, allowing some space underneath to "saw through." So, I lifted the thick end of the tree up on a stump and held it there, while Dad sectioned up the severed pine.

First, he cut it in half, since forty feet at a time seemed a stern enough challenge for a couple of novices. The chainsaw tore into the wood, leaving purposeful cuts in its wake. As Dad proceeded up to the thick end, I was bracing the tree while watching the blue jays dart from tree to tree, enjoying the morning's scavenge, even if it was being altered somewhat by these annoying humans and their loud power tools. The large 20-inch saw made the first few cuts with relative ease, but as Dad approached the thickest part of the tree, the saw was no longer cutting through the wood as easily.

When he got within a couple of feet of the end, Dad leaned on the saw to get maximum penetration. But the log was too thick, and the saw engine labored as the chain spun with minimal progress. Not wanting to overheat the saw and blow an engine, he pulled it from the half-cut groove he had just created. He took a few moments to let the chainsaw cool down a bit as it idled. Satisfied that it (and he) was up to the task again, he hoisted the saw to the cutting position and moved in to finish the job. When he introduced the whirring chain to the log, he didn't quite enter the groove at the same angle. The saw bounced off of the log and recoiled off to his side. That's when my leisurely day in the forest came to an end.

Instantly, the chainsaw made contact with my chin, directly below the left corner of my mouth. It crawled up my face, leaving the corner of my mouth intact, but digging all the way through my cheek and headed toward my left eye.

Fortunately, God (or evolution) provided me with a set of cheek-bones. There are many different uses for a good set of cheekbones, but one of the most important for me on this day was their role in protecting the eye socket. To this day, you can follow the path of that chainsaw on my face as it meets my cheekbone and then deflects farther left, missing the outside corner of my eye by barely an inch, and finally veering back slightly to the right so that my left temple is also spared.

When the accident happened, I didn't scream wildly. I'm not sure I made so much as a shriek. After I fell back, I instinctively covered my face and sat there for a moment somewhat stunned. What had just happened? I had never really seriously considered the damage a chainsaw could do to a body. Not that I thought they were to be trifled with, but I had seen many people use a chainsaw, and I hadn't heard of anyone suffering catastrophic consequences.

Dad knew immediately the situation wasn't good, but with my face in my hands, it was difficult to assess the seriousness of the situation. The blood began to run through my hands and onto my jeans, sig-naling the end of my lumberjacking activities for the day.

After giving Dad and Jim a glimpse of the damage, we decided to use my windbreaker (an old tattered trade union jacket that my Mom had coincidently just washed for the first time in a year) to apply pressure to the wound. I followed Dad to the truck, and he jumped in and began the drive toward a hospital in Boulder, leaving Jim to follow.

While this is a frightening and terrible story up to this point, I can report that the closest I came to dying on this day happened on the trip down the mountain. Dad was understandably frantic and he tried to will the truck back down the winding mountain road at a high rate of speed. He kept asking if I was OK, and kept imploring me to stay awake.

Head wounds are one of the bloodiest injuries a human can suffer, head wounds bleed profusely, but they also tend to stop bleeding faster than a laceration on other parts of the body. By the time we were halfway down the mountain, I was able to pull the windbreaker away from my face enough to realize the flow had stopped. It was at that point I felt confident about my survival.

Regaining a bit of my composure, I realized another danger at hand as dad was doing all he could to get me to the hospital as quickly as possible. We were squealing around the hairpin turns of the canyon, racing toward town. "I'll be fine," I tried to assure him, "if we don't careen off of this mountain before we get to the hospital. Slow down and get both of us there alive!"

When we got down into Boulder it was still only 8 a.m. on a Sunday morning. We had never spent a lot of time in Boulder, so we didn't have a good idea about where the hospital was. At that hour of the morning, there are not a lot of people on the street to ask, either. We did finally find a gas station attendant dutifully preparing to open for the day. Dad pulled over to ask directions to the hospital. Fortunately, Boulder Community Hospital is on a main road, and was not too far from where we stopped to ask for directions.

When we got to the hospital, I walked in behind Dad. It didn't take much to convince the desk nurse I needed some prompt attention. I was immediately directed to a gurney and wheeled into a treatment room.

As I lay there telling my story to a nurse and an orderly, the nurse offered a bit of reassurance. "Today is your lucky day. Dr. Malley will be working on you today, and he is one of the best plastic surgeons around."

Moments later, in came Dr. Malley with the sort of confident swagger which might be offensive at a cocktail party, but was exactly what you want to see in a surgeon who you are trusting to sew your face back together.

The doctor had just finished doing a little plastic surgery work on a late-night car accident victim, and was about ready to head home to enjoy his Sunday. Then I came along to change his plans.

The doctor greeted me, and after a brief assessment of the work before him, he confirmed the nurse's assessment of his confidence. "Don't you worry about a thing. You've got a pro working on you. "

"Mind if I take a few pictures?" he asked, after looking at the exposed wound. "I like to have a set of 'before' and 'after' photos for my book." I never considered how plastic surgeons might need to have a portfolio of their work. I also never dreamed I'd be part of one of those portfolios!

As he pulled out his Polaroid camera and began documenting my situation, he extended me a professional courtesy. "Do you want a set of these for your scrapbook?" It didn't seem right to decline a gesture, and I was a little woozy from the morphine, so I said,

"Sure." My parents took my copy, and forever after, I always found a reason not to look at them. More than three decades later, I have not looked at those pictures, although my Dad keeps them in his bureau to this day.

"You know, I do pretty good work," Dr. Malley said cockily as he continued his preparation. "Are you sure you don't want to watch us work. I can give you a local anesthesia while I sew you up. You can watch in this mirror. You won't feel a thing, I promise."

"No thanks," I replied. "I'm willing to trust your ability on this one. I really don't want to watch you put me back together again."

Within a few moments, I was rolled into surgery and a man came over to place a breathing mask over my face. The serenity of the anesthesia was about to replace this bad dream.

The job of reassembling my face took about four hours. They had to sew three layers of my cheek (from the inside out), and work the best they could around the natural face contours of my chin, mouth cheek, and eyes. Dr. Malley reported that he quit counting at about 250 stitches and guessed that the final total could have been around 400.

By the time I regained consciousness, the Bronco game was over and night was falling. One of the first people I saw when I awoke was Jim DeVaney. My Mom had, of course, rushed to Boulder as soon as she heard the news. But Dad and she had gone down stairs to the cafeteria for a bite to eat when I returned to consciousness.

"Hey, good to see you," Jim said. "You know something? You are very lucky."

That was the first time, with a million to come, that anyone had really called me lucky. In the years since the accident, whenever I tell people the story of the scar on my face, it always ends with somebody saying, "You were very lucky."

I've never really known how to respond to that. If I had truly been lucky, I would have ducked out of the way of the chainsaw in the first place, and I would have gone on to be a television news reporter. But a scar on your cheek generally disqualifies you from that sort of profession. Ever since the accident, I have reveled in telling people, "I now have a face for radio."

But it's hard to dispute that things could have been so much worse. In spite of the indiscriminate nature of a chainsaw's impact against human flesh, the grinding nature of the blade did not adversely impact any of the sensory capacities located on my face. Thirty-five years later, although a couple of nerve endings in the corner of my eye needed rehabilitation, I can still see, smell, hear, feel, and taste with the same acuity as most people in their 50s. Going forward from the incident, I do feel very fortunate.

If the same incident had happened twenty years earlier, doctors may not have had the same positive outlook for the patient in front of them. The use of antibiotics was still in its infancy then. What's more, I happen to be allergic to penicillin, so if substitutes (which only came onto the scene in the 1950s) had not been available in 1978, I might have been in a difficult spot.

Additionally, I suffered from the cultural effect of being a 17-year-old American teenager. I was not particularly unique, but kids on the cusp of adulthood in the United States are generally the vainest beings on the face of the Earth. Your looks are about all you have at that point in your life. Homecoming and Senior Prom loom as far more important than they rightly deserve. It's your last chance to live up to the "Breakfast Club" label you may have been given (or earned), or to overcome it. In my mind, I would always be remembered after this incident, for a scar. Indeed, many of my high school classmates were unable to have a relationship with me after this incident. I understand the reflex. People who remind us that we aren't invincible are sometimes uncomfortable to be around. I've felt the feeling myself as I've met different people through the course of my life.

However, others drew closer, and watching the sociological experiment happening before me every day was enlightening. I sensed in many ways, it was the people who might have a little scarring of their own (maybe in a less visible place), who made it a point to be supportive. Under the façade of our superficial selves *do* exist vulnerable and caring human beings. Too often, though, we must have a personal relationship with tragedy before we can truly be compassionate toward others. I wouldn't have learned that fact as quickly, had I not endured my encounter with a chainsaw.

Moving forward, I could have used the scar on my face as an excuse for not pursuing my way in life. I could have felt sorry for myself and wallowed in alcohol and self-pity. Frankly, it was nip-and-tuck on a couple of occasions, but in the end, it just didn't seem the most productive use of this most amazing coincidence of being alive on this small planet out near the end of the Milky Way Galaxy.

While we all have our own crosses to bear, I still feel angry when I think of the scores of talented people who have wasted the amazing talent they were given by killing themselves through their self-indulgences. There is an endless, and growing, list of public figures who have caved in under pressure (both real and imagined) to pursue a life dominated by drugs, alcohol, fast cars and a reckless lifestyle. Mankind is worse off for every waste of talent.

Somehow, though, I found a path to healing which came with the clarity of mind to understand the sort of torture this situation presented for my dad. As I have become a father myself, I know the heartache of seeing your child injured. And I can imagine the guilt and self-loathing that could follow if your child were injured at your own hand. An early appreciation of those feelings motivated me to persevere.

Early on, I knew that between my dad and me, I had the easier job. I just had to get better and carry on with my life. To the extent that I could be successful, Dad could jettison the heavy burden of guilt he had heaped upon himself. If I wallowed, his pain and suffering would be doubled.

Fortunately, I never was the type to spend a lot of time in front of a mirror, and the scar eventually faded into more of a historical footnote, so I found it pretty easy to face life as if I was never injured. However, early on, I had to adjust to people who saw the "new me" for the first time.

Even now, as the scar has faded over the past three decades, someone I have known for a while, will suddenly "see" the scar. I can see the look of someone taken aback by the discovery. Sometimes they ask to hear the story. Sometimes they try to pretend they didn't notice. I'm sure I've been passed over for a few jobs by employers who thought a scar-faced representative of their organization was not the image they were looking to portray. Working in the public relations business, image is thought to be everything. Companies want to put their best foot (and face) forward.

But I simply could not allow other people's perception to get me down. I played varsity baseball the following spring, and received honorable mention on the all-city team as an outfielder. I graduated from high school and then college. I got married and had children. I have worked as a writer for a number of organizations for nearly thirty years, and I've generally had a successful life.

If I had stumbled and wallowed over the past three decades, would people consider me nearly as lucky? Is it the circumstances that make luck, or is it the response to an obstacle that makes the luck flow? Do we make our own luck, or is there a cosmic scoreboard tracking your actions and determining whether today will be your lucky day?

Spending a couple of weeks attending school looking like the Elephant Man was not how I would have written the senior year of high school in my life's script. But the balance of my young life was the gift I received in return. I deeply appreciate the opportunity to continue on with life, despite the nicks and scars and allergies that come with it, and I've always felt driven to make the most of it and look for ways to improve the character I am playing. Am I lucky to have found the inner peace and strength to move forward with life? I suppose, but I don't know for sure. It could be I was just stubborn.

After all, what *IS* luck?

CHAPTER 3

WHERE DID LUCK COME FROM IN OUR LANGUAGE?

"The meeting of preparation with opportunity generates the offspring we call luck."

— Tony Robbins

Luck is a fascinating word, which is not any better defined when you attempt to mine for the origin of the word. The concept of luck is something to which people in all cultures have tried to ascribe, but describing it has become a more ticklish matter. Perhaps that is why there are so many synonyms for the concept.

To mine for the origin of the concept, I thought I would look at the etymology of the word itself. It provided some clues, but since I believe luck is a concept humankind has been grasping for since the Neanderthal era, tracing "luck" back to the Dark Ages doesn't tell the whole story. However, it provides a colorful entry in the Online Etymology Dictionary.

(Online Etymology Dictionary searching "luck" at www.etymonline.com)

luck (v.)

> *by 1945, from luck (n.). To luck out "succeed through luck" is American English colloquial, attested by 1946; to luck into (something good) is from 1944. However, lukken was a verb in Middle English (mid-15c.) meaning "to happen, chance;" also, "happen fortunately."*

luck (n.)

> *late 15c. from early Middle Dutch luc, shortening of gheluc "happiness, good fortune," of unknown origin. It has cognates in Dutch geluk, Middle High German g(e)lücke, German Glück "fortune, good luck." Perhaps first borrowed in English as a gambling term. To be down on (one's) luck is from 1832; to be in luck is from 1900; to push (one's) luck is from 1911. Good luck as a salutation to one setting off to do something is from 1805. The expression better luck next time was documented in 1802. A gentleman was lately walking through St Giles's, where a leveling citizen attempted to pick his pocket of a handkerchief, which the gentleman caught in time, and secured, observing to the fellow, that he had missed his aim, the latter, with perfect sang-froid, answered, "better luck next time master." ["Monthly Mirror," London, 1802]*

chance (n.)

*c.1300, "something that takes place, what happens, an occur-rence" (good or bad, but more often bad), from Old French cheance "accident, chance, fortune, luck, situation, the fall-ing of dice" (12c., Modern French chance), from Vulgar Latin *cadentia "that which falls out," a term used in dice, from neu-ter plural of Latin cadens, present participle of cadere "to fall."*

In English frequently in the plural, chances. The word's notions of "opportunity" and "randomness" are as old as the record of it in English and now all but crowd out the word's original notion of "mere occurrence." Main chance "thing of most importance" is from 1570s, bearing the older sense. The mathematical (and hence odds-making) sense is attested from 1778. To stand a chance (or not) is from 1796.

To take (one's) chances "accept what happens" (early 14c.) is from the old, neutral sense; to take a chance/take chances is originally (by 1814) "participate in a raffle or lottery or game;" extended sense of "take a risk" is by 1826.

hap (n.)

*c.1200, "chance, a person's luck, fortune, fate;" also "unforeseen occurrence," from Old Norse happ "chance, good luck," from Proto-Germanic *khapan (source of Old English gehæp "conve-nient, fit"), from PIE *kob- "to suit, fit, succeed" (cf. Old Church Slavonic kobu "fate, foreboding, omen," Old Irish cob "victory"). Meaning "good fortune" is from early 13c.*

swastika (n.)

Greek cross with arms bent at right angles, 1871 (later specifically as emblem of the Nazi party, 1932), from Sanskrit svastika-s, literally "being fortunate," from svasti-s "well-being, luck," from su- "well" + as-, root of asti "(he) is," from root of Latin esse "to be" (see essence). Also known as gammadion (Byzantine), cross cramponnee (heraldry), Thor's hammer, and, perhaps, fylfot. Originally an ancient cosmic or religious symbol thought to bring good luck. Use in reference to the Nazi emblem first recorded in English in 1932. The German word was Hakenkreuz, literally "hook-cross."

infelicity (n.)

late 14c., from Latin infelicitas "ill luck, misfortune," from infelix (genitive infelicis) "unfruitful, barren; unfortunate, unhappy, causing misfortune, unlucky," from in- "not, opposite of" (see in- (1)) + felix (see felicity).

adventure (n.)

c.1200, auenture "that which happens by chance, fortune, luck," from Old French aventure (11c.) "chance, accident, occurrence, event, happening," from Latin adventura (res) "(a thing) about to happen," from adventurus, future participle of advenire "to come to, reach, arrive at," from ad- "to" (see ad-) + venire "to come" (see venue).

Meaning developed through "risk/danger" (a trial of one's chances), c.1300, and "perilous undertaking" (late 14c.) and thence to "a novel or exciting incident" (1560s). Earlier it also meant "a won-

der, a miracle; accounts of marvelous things" (13c.). The -d- was restored 15c.-16c. Venture is a 15c. variant.

albatross (n.)

1670s, probably from Spanish or Portuguese alcatraz "pelican" (16c.), perhaps derived from Arabic al-ghattas "sea eagle" [Barnhart]; or from Portuguese alcatruz "the bucket of a water wheel" [OED], from Arabic al-qadus "machine for drawing water, jar" (from Greek kados "jar"), in reference to the pelican's pouch (cf. Arabic saqqa "pelican," literally "water carrier"). Either way, the spelling was influenced by Latin albus "white." The name was extended, through some mistake, by English sailors to a larger sea-bird (order Tubinares).

Albatrosses were considered good luck by sailors; figurative sense of "burden" (1936) is from Coleridge's "Rime of the Ancient Mariner" (1798) about the bad luck of a sailor who shoots an albatross and then is forced to wear its corpse as an indication that he, not the whole ship, offended against the bird. The prison-island of Alcatraz in San Francisco Bay is named for pelicans that roosted there.

hoodoo (n.)

"one who practices voodoo," 1870, American English, probably an alteration of voodoo. Meaning "something that causes or brings bad luck" is attested from 1880."

We have assigned luck to inanimate objects, other animals and symbols, in an effort to "get in front" of luck's fickle finger, but we are eternally left to pick up the pieces, and define our own relative good fortune, after our life's shifts "hit the fan."

The concept of luck, under other names and descriptions, is probably as old as our species. You can imagine early humans celebrating an abundant hunting or harvesting season. But without the benefit of farming tools or firearms, there were more things beyond their control. Many rituals were performed in the interest of trying to persuade the spirits of good fortune favorably. Some of these rituals were probably helpful toward the effectiveness of the hunting party (sharpening your spears together might assure cross-checks of the weaponry), and some just helped build community (conducting a spirit dance prior to sending out the hunters). Whatever has happened over the history of these rituals (and probably still does in hunting camps around the world), most cultures have always made sure to give thanks to their Creator in the process somewhere. Whether or not the Creator is there to hear our humble pleas, it seems like too big of an item to overlook, if He or She *really is* paying attention. So let's dance!

Much of luck's linguistic trail, as a word, is traced back into the Dark Ages of the 10th through 12th centuries. The English description of the phenomenon seems to be drawn from German origins.

That luck's origins seem to emanate from the Dark Ages is also not very surprising. With conquering hoards moving across Europe from different directions in an alternating sequence, and pandemic diseases caused by invisible bacteria and viruses sweeping across the villages at the time, it is easy to imagine how such misfortunes would send people searching for reason. Beyond reason, people would subscribe to anything they thought might improve their dismal plight.

Why has this death and carnage come to our people? How is it that one family is decimated by disease, while another escapes relatively unscathed? It must be the result of how they are living, they reasoned. But with the source of their disease still invisible to a civilization that would not accept the existence of microscopic bacteria until the end of the 19th century, they had to assign a cause for the suffering. If there is no visible reason for the differences, there must be something else making a difference. "Hey, those people hang a clove of garlic over their doorway. That must be good luck!"

Luck, in some incarnations, became something to be feared. Those who seemed to attain a level of control over their luck often came under suspicion. At a certain point in American history, people stood accused of being witches and were burned. Of course, in that instance, the pendulum of luck swung quickly away from the accused, as the early methods of justice made it difficult to prove beyond a doubt that they were not witches.

Many Native American tribes embraced the prospect of controlling the unknown by turning to their medicine man, partly for the tonic to cure what ailed them, and partly to engage the Good Spirits to look over their future pursuits. Other than the Chief himself, there were few people more respected in the Native American culture than the medicine man, or "shaman." Anyone who seemed to control the invisible forces of fate was certainly someone who commanded our respect.

While much of human history ebbed and flowed upon the brute military powers of the nations involved, almost no physical human conflict has ever been fought without combatants from both sides calling upon all manner of "lucky" forces to see them through the skirmish.

Luck is a concept that has also been glorified and polished for the purposes of promoting the gaming industry throughout the world. Luck, as a term, is perhaps most used today to describe an experience in a game of chance, whether it is betting on a football game or a horse race, or spending an evening at the casino, or simply plopping down a few dollars on the Powerball.

No matter the challenge before us, we are all looking for a positive result in this difficult and complicated world. To achieve that result, we are willing to try just about anything. Even if we are not sure of the cause-and-effect nature of the cure, can we stand to take the chance of turning our backs on what could be a difference maker? Can we leave any stone unturned in our pursuit of some good luck?

CHAPTER 4

WHAT IS LUCK?

"Everything in life is luck."

—Donald Trump

As I was raised to do when looking for the definition of a word, I turn to our friends at Merriam Webster to define luck the best way they know how:

> "1 *a :* a force that brings good fortune or adversity
>   *b :* the events or circumstances that operate for or against an individual
> 2: favoring chance; *also : success <had great luck growing orchids>*"

By permission. From *Merriam-Webster's Collegiate® Dictionary, 11ᵗʰ Edition* ©2014 by Merriam-Webster, Inc. (www.Merriam-Webster.com).

Wikipedia gives us a little deeper view into the etymology and definition of luck:

*"**Luck** When thought of as a factor beyond one's control, without regard to one's will, intention, or desired result. There are at least two senses people usually mean when they use the term, the prescriptive sense and the descriptive sense. In the prescriptive sense, luck is a supernatural and deterministic concept that there are forces (e.g. gods or spirits) which prescribe that certain events occur very much the way laws of physics will prescribe that certain events occur. It is the prescriptive sense that people mean when they say they "do not believe in luck". In the descriptive sense, luck is a word people give after the occurrence of events which they find to be fortuitous or unfortuitous, and maybe improbable. "*

The text above is taken from Wikipedia Encyclopedia
(http://en.wikipedia.org/wiki/Luck)

Luck's definitions leave us with a wide array of examples, and circumstances by which it came to be defined, but it rarely addresses the source(s). Remember, we are trying to describe an element that works behind the scenes. We mostly do not know when luck is present, and we certainly cannot ascertain its motives, until after it has left its mark. As was suggested earlier, luck appears to be more of a force than it is matter. Is there any way to harness this force? As mankind has studied the properties of gravity and centrifuge, and we have learned to use those forces to manage our world. Perhaps the same can become true with the fates. At least, we are eternally hoping so.

Essentially the phenomenon of luck is broken into two primary categories. Things that happen completely by chance, and things that happen due to forces in the universe (whether that be from a God force, witchcraft, the pull of the planets, or ourselves).

Whichever side of this debate you come down on, it is clear we often have very little say in which way our luck will fall. Because the human species is endlessly curious, there have been efforts to understand these forces, with the goal of being able to anticipate our fates a little better. But anyone who tells you they have the formula for how fate works is probably looking to sell it to you in a snake oil bottle at the county fair.

Humans are unique and often unpredictable animals. As we mentioned earlier, your journey through this life is uniquely your own. There are currently more than seven billion unique journeys going on around you on this Earth, each with a unique and unpredictable human at the controls. Some of them are completely despicable. Others can warm your heart on a cold winter's day. All of this makes prognostication very complicated.

Among the academic psychologists, and others who have studied the phenomenon of luck, the origins have generally been broken into four different sources. Divine intervention, luck as a response to life's choices, responses to the physical forces of nature, and pure dumb luck.

Divine interventionists postulate either everything is predetermined (and thus we have no real control over the events in our lives), or there is a Heavenly accounting for our actions, which dictates whether something good or bad will happen to a person in a given situation. "He got just what he deserved," is a common refrain, whether the result was positive or negative. Nearly every religion promotes the notion that good deeds will beget a positive result for the future. Negative deeds, conversely, will result in negative results in the future—even if the come-uppance waits until Judgment Day.

The people who believe **luck happens in response to your own life choices** are usually quite practical about the fates. While there may be a number of 50-50 situations in life, where fate could fall either way, there are also ways in which you can stay out of—or get into—situations where the odds are against you. What you put into a situation, these people would say, has a direct bearing on what you get out of it.

Luck resulting from **responses to the physical forces of nature** captures the influences of the moon and the stars (as in astrology), but also entertains Earthly forces which come to bear in crystal balls, customers' palms, and Tarot cards. People's view of the weather, and how it affects their behavior and outlook, will also be considered here. In Nebraska, it is a part of the culture to expect a whopper of a storm to come on the heels of several beautiful weather days. It is just an accepted, standing obligation to pay back the "system" for its blue-sky favors.

And then there is **dumb luck**. In the world of chance, these are situations we have no real opportunity to anticipate prior to their appearance. The "chips fall where they may," and if the hurricane blows an uprooted tree in your direction, whether it hits or misses you is a matter of dumb luck. Over time, we may discover our luck wasn't as dumb as it seemed, but at the time of the incident, your fate is out of your hands and into the winds.

Let's take a deeper look at each of these four origins of luck.

CHAPTER 5

LUCK FROM THE HEAVENS ABOVE

"Indeed, none but the Deity can tell what is good luck and what is bad before the returns are all in."

— Mark Twain, in a letter to Samuel Moffett, 6 August 1904

God's Role in Our Fortunes

"You have to participate relentlessly in the manifestation of your own blessings."

— Elizabeth Gilbert

Using the context in which most human understandings have been built, I suspect the initial concept of luck was expressed through the term "blessings." "To be blessed" means "to be favored by God." Blessings, therefore, are directly associated with God and come from God.

I wince every time I hear a professional athlete say in a post-game interview, "I give my glory to God for all of the blessings he has bestowed upon us tonight." Aren't there athletes in the opposing locker room who have committed equally as much energy exhorting God to favor them? It also occurs to me that these people are selling their own abilities short, by implying that without God they could never have achieved this victory. Many times, those "glory to God" athletes find themselves at the podium because the ball bounced one way instead of the other. Godly interference is the only reliable explanation for why a basketball will hit off the flange of the rim, bounce straight up in the air, and return to the rim, where it will either find a way in, or rattle out of the cylinder. If those sorts of shots start going in for you on a disproportionate basis, people *are* going to be very interested in your relationship with the Higher Powers.

When a series of good events happen to us over time, we tend to think God is smiling upon us. But maybe the circumstances were just right and we were lucky enough to be in the right place at the right time—and to perform in the clutch. Of course, we have to accomplish several intermediate steps to be in a position to "receive God's blessing" by making the pivotal shot. The long process of climbing our way up the ladder to the big game always takes a lot more hard work and determination than luck. The physical ability, endurance, and mental focus to be able to attain our goals are part of our DNA, and could be credited to God's complicated plan of bestowing individual attributes to people . . . or just to the chemical wonder of the DNA.

God has always been a convenient way to explain things that are relatively unexplainable. Because we can't explain it, we can't disprove that God IS at the source of all twists of fate. Where lies the burden of proof in this case? Of course, the Holy interference in human affairs also tends to minimize the chance and randomness of luck. There are still religious sorts in our population who believe nothing happens without the influence of a higher power. The Puritans came to America in the 16th and 17th centuries with a strong sense of predestination. While this gives us some comfort in the larger world, it is a stretch to imagine that God has a hand in all of our chance encounters in life.

Flip a coin ten times. Some of you will turn seven or eight "heads," while others may get that many "tails." But those extreme cases will balance each other out, and most of us will get four, five, or six "heads" or "tails." Adhering to the system of divine intervention, only God knows which one of you will turn up seven "heads" before you start flipping. How much minutia can one Divine power handle? Does God really care about the outcome of your coin-flipping exercise?

Yet, when we are in desperate need of a positive turn in our lives, so many of us still turn to the Lord above in the form of prayer. We pray for good health. We pray for answers to the questions in our lives for which we can find no easy solution. Many of us even pray for others, and their life challenges. Sometimes those prayers appear to be answered. Sometimes, they are not—at least as far as we can tell.

"God has a bigger plan," is the conciliatory plea we all turn to when our prayers are not answered satisfactorily. When someone close to us passes away, we shift gears and pray for a happy resolution in the after-life.

I very much appreciate that the universe is infinitely more complicated than any one of us could fully understand. Every religion has its "after-life" story, and if my particular version of Heaven—and how you gain admission—is correct, I am comforted by what awaits us in the hereafter. But none of us knows. Perhaps God will exclude the infidels among us, and only be welcoming Jews, or Catholics, or Muslims, or Missouri Synod Lutherans. I personally believe God does not care through which human prophet you are delivered to Him/Her. But many people here on Earth will tell you differently. That's why they call it faith.

But maybe, when we pray, we are just not being specific enough. Maybe we just assume God knows what we are asking for, without being explicit in our pleas.

When I was a young, testosterone-laden lad, I must I admit I occasionally prayed to find myself in the middle of a car wash full of cheerleaders. It was the 1970s, and the movie "Car Wash" had come out to show us that the car wash was a great place to make friends and pick up a date.

This particular prayer came nowhere close to coming true during my high school years. It was only answered many years later—as a parent volunteer for my daughter's cheerleading squad fundraiser. I really never thought, as part of my fantasy, that my role at the car wash would be to keep track of the money and turn on the faucet at the bank (which was gracious enough to donate its lot for the activity), and make sure all of the creepy fellows didn't spend too much time leering at the girls.

"What are you looking at? Keep moving."

I must say, if God was answering my prayer twenty-five years later, He has quite an ironic sense of humor.

It is the ultimate moment of faith when, after the fates have been decided, we reflect on what happened and determine whether God answered our prayer. Sometimes it takes a little reconstruction of history to complete the circuit. Or, other times, we merely resign ourselves to the fact that God may well have responded to the situation we brought to His attention, but it may have happened in a way that we do not understand. Be careful what you ask for, and how you ask for it.

Maybe God is working on a bigger plan that trumps our trivial pleas for help. Because most of us do not have a direct line to the Big Guy, we cannot know with certainty. We simply have to believe.

This blind belief has proven dangerous over the course of human existence. Various civilizations have felt compelled to offer sacrifices to the Gods in exchange for the future success of the whole. For some people, it has been limited to sacrificing farm animals. For others, sacrificing human virgins was the standard. Most of us in the 21st century would concur that human (and probably even animal) sacrifice is a misguided, masochistic approach. But there are still religions that promote the killing of other humans as a practical necessity to give glory to their Gods. The relationship between humans and their Gods invites such atrocities as flying planes into the World Trade Center and driving bomb-laden vehicles into a crowd of people in search of God's glory.

Other than praying for good luck in a crisis situation—or a delivery into Heaven, people in our society also pray to maintain the relationship with their Creator. Sometimes, through prayer, we are just performing maintenance on our relationship with the Almighty. Maintaining our relationship with God causes many thousands of churches to fill their pews on a weekly basis. The millions of dollars collected by televangelists over the years depend on this maintenance. Whether you pray through the television, at church, or by your bedside stand, daily prayers continue to be a part of many people's lives. The daily prayer ritual serves as a way to keep our mental perspective on things.

The Lord's Prayer, displayed in so many homes and hearts, attempts to frame a solid daily perspective—along with a little deference to the Almighty.

> *Our Father, which art in heaven,*
> *Hallowed be thy Name.*
> *Thy Kingdom come.*
> *Thy will be done on earth,*
> *As it is in heaven.*
> *Give us this day our daily bread.*
> *And forgive us our trespasses,*
> *As we forgive those who trespass against us.*

And lead us not into temptation,
But deliver us from evil.
For thine is the kingdom,
The power, and the glory,
For ever and ever.
Amen.

The Serenity Prayer is also a humble plea for perspective in this complicated world. In the context of these prayers, perhaps our pleas to our Maker are akin to self-reflection. Instead of asking for a particular favor, perhaps we are merely asking for the power to consider everything and make the best choices available to us.

God grant me the serenity
To accept the things I cannot change;
Courage to change the things I can;
And wisdom to know the difference.

Living one day at a time;
Enjoying one moment at a time;
Accepting hardships as the pathway to peace;
Taking, as He did, this sinful world
As it is, not as I would have it;
Trusting that He will make all things right
If I surrender to His Will;
So that I may be reasonably happy in this life
And supremely happy with Him
Forever and ever in the next.
Amen.

This maintenance of our godly connection is soothing, but as we extend this God force into the specifics of our lives, can we reasonably expect intervention on the smaller things before us?

Does God really have a stake in whether I choose the correct size of wrench to turn the bolt before me? Is it his will that I should shuffle through the tool box each and every time to find the 3/8 box wrench instead of the 7/16th or the 5/16th? Is He really at the track when I choose to bet $2 on Lucky Boy in the seventh race?

Does God decide whether I turn in to that pub for a cold one with my friends, or go straight home to help manage the affairs on the home front? Does God decide that certain people always end up with an abusive spouse? (Let me say, for the record, that my wife is the most amazing woman I have ever been associated with and she would never strike me in anger. However, if I chose to pull into the pub more often in the future, she might be justifiably compelled to reconsider!)

At a certain point, many people become incredulous of the notion that God is involved in every breath from every animal on this and other Earths. We have certainly been bestowed an amazing world in which to propagate our species. However, as the world unfolded, it has done so amidst a society that, while we have plenty of problems, has developed transportation, medical, and technological infrastructures to extend our reach into the corners of our own globe, and into the distant reaches of our solar system. Even if you believe God created all we see, is he really micromanaging every turn of fate?

Crediting or blaming God for our luck seems like an overly simplistic view to explain away the wins and losses in our lives. Of course, the very concept of an omnipresent God is larger than most of us can truly comprehend, anyway, so who among us would be willing to suggest a micromanaging Supreme Being could not exist? Can there be something beyond your ability to physically witness? My religious upbringing suggests there is, but it doesn't speak to who shall winneth the seventh race at Arlington—or who will reign victorious at this year's Super Bowl. I guess God Almighty doesn't want to spoil it for us by telling us the outcome beforehand.

Do human problems come about because people aren't able to fit into God's "system," or is it that the "systems" do not fully account for all of the possible combinations that the nature of the human species can present? It seems arrogant to assume that humans will automatically reprogram themselves to work within the context of "the system." But if you want your driver's license, court documents, or your free government cheese, most of us will grudgingly get in line, or take a number, and wait to be called.

Much of this discussion can be boiled down to a fundamental question of philosophy: Do you believe that the universe is orderly and humanity brings chaos to it? Or do you believe that the universe is a chaotic place and the human species has a need to devise its own societal order amidst the chaos? No matter the source, if our world has a degree of chaos, doesn't luck automatically become a part of the equation in each of our relative levels of success?

We have discovered a number of physical orderly properties about our universe which we can define (i.e. the speed of light, properties of gravity, etc.), which would lead you to believe that there is some order within the cosmos. But is that order merely the set of physical limitations in the void of space without any particular interrelationship with other particles, matter, or situations? What if light traveled at a different speed closer to the center of the galaxy?

Because I can happily state that an asteroid has not come forth and destroyed this happy little Earth we live on, I believe we should express our gratitude to the creator of our world (just in case he IS on the job) for shielding us from collisions with other worlds, rendering both worlds lifeless. But when our "luck" runs out and an asteroid does take aim on our home planet, praise to our Creator for the atmospheric shield is probably going to dry up.

Perhaps the laws of physics are ultimately so precise, that everything is calculated to happen in a predetermined sequence. Perhaps it was the Higher Powers who created, and set into motion, all of the laws of physics in the first place.

I still cling to the notion that humans are more than obedient atoms in the vast universe. We are unique thinkers. We have people among us who relish making a conscious decision to take "the road less traveled." What happens to that set of physical laws when the particles under its influence begin to think and act for themselves? The unpredictable pops up. Something that could never be imagined happens. Good things and bad things begin to occur and develop as we alter the course of how we do things.

We have discovered a wide range of minerals and chemicals as a human race, and nearly all of them have created an impact on our society. Sometimes, it is many years before we determine the dangerous nature of the items we are using. Asbestos was a marvelous invention, both for its insulation qualities and for its fire-retardant reputation. But thousands of people have died from overexposure to it in shipyards, or on construction and roofing crews, or working in the heating and cooling business. Lead has many useful qualities, but it turns out to be toxic when ingested by the human body.

I can see the Supreme Being getting befuddled by all of our independent thinking and putting us all on pause to proclaim, "Whoa there! All bets are off if these little creations of mine are going to start acting irrationally and doing what they darned well please. If those people aren't going to play by the rules I set up, I am washing my hands of this entire experiment." Perhaps all of the mathematical calculations have been established to determine the speed and power of inanimate forces, but when you add the complication of free-thinking beings into the equation, many of the constants are thrown off. The more brain function the animals attain in this terrarium called Earth, the less anyone can predict the final results.

Imagine, too, the complexities of an Almighty who must determine the outcome of every situation, given that he may be receiving millions of different prayers exhorting Him to bring about conflicting outcomes to any given situation. Several members of Al-Qaeda may be praying for deliverance from the infidels, who may at the same time, be praying for deliverance from the terrors inflicted by Al-Qaeda. Nearly every military struggle in human existence has seen combatants from both sides praying to God (though sometimes varying prophets) for diametrically opposite results.

I may be praying for the grace of God to shine upon me as I attempt to get hired for a particular position. But the other four finalists may also be bidding his help in securing the same job.

Is my God better than their God? How is an Almighty to respond? Perhaps his preordained plan for us trumps any individual plea He may receive.

I suspect the answer to the earlier philosophical question of "chaos vs. order" is that we live in a world of both orderly and chaotic properties. Humans live within that world and bring their own versions of both order and chaos into the chemistry with their existence.

That definition sets the stage for a complicated matrix of possibilities, and as such, opens the door for people to see the many ways in which they are fortunate.

Often, when I don't receive what I was praying for, it has ended up being a very good thing over the long haul. What we want and what we need are distinctly different (at least that's what my mother told me). But it becomes seemingly impossible to distinguish the differences between "want" and "need" for ourselves sometimes. It is much easier for our own personal sense of accountability to defer every result to the will of God. There is so much less for us to fret and worry over if we can turn all our troubles over to a Higher Power.

My Protestant upbringing suggests that "cleansing" the sinner's soul is not only possible, it is necessary for acceptance into Heaven. But each religious flavor has a wide array of other devout practices, which apparently increase your favor with God. Much of the pomp and ceremony are lost on me. I understand the power of legacy and shared rituals. I just don't know if your fate in this life, or in an afterlife, is determined by your strict adherence to these rituals.

For all I know, in the end, the ritual participation quotient could be the deciding factor for who gets through the Pearly Gates. And if it is, I may need to make plans to be doing something else with my after-life.

Depending on whom we talk to, people may well consider divine intervention as a physical force. Others frame God's role in our lives as reactionary (if we behave according to the Commandments, we can expect to have things go well for us, but if we don't . . .). I have chosen to keep it separate because there are many other physical forces to which we credit our success, or blame our failures. Let's look at those.

REFLECTION QUESTIONS

How much of a role do you believe God plays in our day-to-day fates?

Does God influence every outcome directly—no matter how small?

How do we justify promoting one religious belief over another, even to the extent of condemning others to death (either now or in the after-life) if they don't share our beliefs?

BEING FORTUNATE

<u>fortune (n.)</u>

c.1300, "chance, luck as a force in human affairs," from Old French fortune "lot, good fortune, misfortune" (12c.), from Latin fortuna "chance, fate, good luck," from fors (genitive fortis) "chance, luck," possibly from PIE *bhrtu- and related to base *bher- (1) "to carry" (see infer).

Often personified as a goddess; her wheel betokens vicissitude. Sense of "owned wealth" first found in Spenser; probably it evolved from senses of "one's condition or standing in life," hence "position as determined by wealth," then "wealth" itself. Soldier of fortune first attested 1660s. Fortune 500 "most profitable American companies" is 1955, from the list published annually in "Fortune" magazine.

http://www.etymonline.com/index.php
?term=fortune&allowed_in_frame=0

"I never complained of the vicissitudes of fortune, nor suffered my face to be overcast at the revolution of the heavens, except once, when my feet were bare, and I had not the means of obtaining shoes. I came to the chief of Kufah in a state of much dejection, and saw there a man who had no feet. I returned thanks to God and acknowledged his mercies, and endured my want of shoes with patience."

The Gulistan, or Rose Garden
Sa'di (pen name of Muslih-ud-Din, Persian poet ca. 1184-1291)

Both the Greeks (Tyche) and the Romans (Fortuna), assigned goddesses to the work of managing our good (bona) and bad (mala) fortunes. As goddesses, they have been depicted in many different ways, often possessing a wheel, which is supposed to depict a balance between good and bad fates in our lives.

"Sometimes (Fortuna) is (depicted as) blind, as an acknowledgment that good luck does not always come to those who seem to most deserve it; at other times She is described as having wings, much like many Etruscan goddesses—and indeed She was equated with the old Etruscan Fate Goddess Nortia, who was often shown winged."

From: The Obscure Goddess Online Directory
http://www.thaliatook.com/OGOD/fortuna.html

Assigning our fates to the gods is certainly not a new phenomenon. The Greeks and the Romans were among the most successful civilizations in assigning their fates to a broad panel of god-like figures, each responsible for particular areas of our existences. Catholics also attempt to lighten God's load by using the patron saint system of issue management.

Many Romans offered praise to Goddess Fortuna for the position to which they were born in the world, almost no matter where they landed on the social ladder. Thus, our modern notion of "being fortunate" was born.

No matter the source of our fortune, there is no denying you are fortunate if you have the time to read a book, in a country that doesn't censor very much of what is written in the world. Still, many people do not take advantage of the good fortune of living in a free country with a broad array of reading materials. Some can't even read. Others read just enough to get them into situations which ultimately prove overwhelming. If only they had read the fine print.

I have worked at the side of many organizational leaders, and I can tell you I do not often envy those whom many others would describe as "most fortunate." Issues and problems come at leaders from every direction. They spend longer hours on the job (or in work-related chores), which causes them to spend many nights away (or mentally detached) from home. Sometimes the issues rise to a level in which the leaders begin losing sleep thinking about it. Their final decision and any important issue may serve as the pivotal point for the future of the organization. And yet, many people would describe them as fortunate. Even the leaders themselves often admit they are very fortunate, if only for the executive-level paycheck.

There have been several occasions in which I've watched a top executive unravel (live, or via television or internet), and I felt fortunate to have a job that allowed me some balance. I have learned that fortune is not necessarily the position in life where you land, but it comes from finding a position from which you can thrive and use your talents to the fullest. If that happens in a place and time where your skill is needed and appreciated, you are the "most fortunate."

Abraham Lincoln was, at his core, a bit of a tortured soul. Born on the western edge of the new American colonies, he suffered many defeats in his lifetime. Even when circumstances smiled upon him, allowing him to ascend to the role of President of the United States, he faced the dire situation of a nation divided. He spent most of his time as commander-in-chief presiding over a Civil War, which represented the darkest and bloodiest four years in our nation's history. Until Barack Obama (another Illinois senator who became President), no leader of this country had been so roundly accused of treason and treachery toward his own country. Then, just as the war was finally subsiding and Lincoln could begin to see the opportunity to attend to some of the more pleasant aspects of being President (not to mention the monumental task of Reconstruction), he was assassinated.

On any list ranking of presidents, Lincoln is considered among the best this country has ever had. And yet, he was tortured throughout the duration of his service by a war that pitted brothers against brothers. Blood was spilled by the gallons during each year of his presidency. All he really had to show for his term in office was the Emancipation Proclamation (which did not make African Americans significantly free in this country for more than 100 years after its adoption), the Gettysburg Address, and a traumatized widow left to raise fatherless sons.

His talents came to the fore at a time when his country was in dire need. He reshaped the future of the United States of America, but at great personal cost. Was Lincoln really fortunate? As a country, I believe the United States was fortunate Abraham Lincoln arrived at the White House at the point in history he did, but the Lincoln family would be right to feel the sting of his unfortunate timing.

Even if you happen to be born into a family of fortune, it has been proven time and again to not necessarily be a fortunate thing. Do a

Google search on Edsel Ford, or King Edward VIII of England. Just being born into the lap of privilege does not guarantee you a happy existence on this Earth.

"I'm fortunate to be here tonight," is a pretty funny opening for a performer, because like all comedy, it has a kernel of a truth to which we can relate. We are all fortunate to be where we are today. I was born in the United States of America, and I feel infinitely more fortunate for that twist of chemical fate. I had two loving parents who, despite difficulties, stayed together until death did they part. My mother mostly stayed home and played the role of housewife to five rambunctious kids. Parents and siblings loved me and raised me into what I have become. For that, more than any other game of chance, I feel most fortunate. Really nothing else has made as much of a difference in how I turned out.

I feel fortunate that I was the first-born, but others in line may well feel quite content with their position in the birth order. That's OK. We all have to come to grips with the cards life has dealt in our direction. If you can count those things as fortunate developments, it helps you move forward.

In many ways, I was fortunate to both be involved in, and to have survived, my chainsaw encounter. I was fortunate it happened in 1978, when plastic surgery had a little bit of history to draw on, and the surgeons had a little knowledge base available to know what to do when a kid makes hamburger out of his face. As I mentioned earlier, I also feel incredibly fortunate I survived the incident with my mouth, nose, ears, and eyes all in the same basic shape.

I was also fortunate for the reality check it provided to me. As a senior in high school, it really could not have been timed better. I found out which friends cared about the human behind Brian's face, and who cared about something else. Karen Olson and Janet Leasher in particular, took me under their wing and we became even better friends throughout the balance of my senior year.

It wasn't that their instincts to "pity the leper" were kicking in. They just knew the kid behind the face, and took it upon themselves to make sure I didn't get lost. I am eternally indebted to those two, for being who they were (and are). In many ways, the accident provided me a quick test to see who was dealing with my face and who was dealing with the person behind it. That lesson endured for many years as I met new professors and bosses, and people on the street.

There are other fortuitous things about my physical characteristics and abilities with which I have been born. I was gifted with just enough athletic and intellectual ability to hold my own across a broad range of sports, hobbies and interests. In an effort to try to participate in a wide variety of experiences, I have not zealously committed myself to being an expert at very many of them. Since I wasn't likely to make a living as an athlete, I was forced to develop other skills in order to make a living for this life of mine.

I am fortunate to have an iron stomach, and am generally resistant to much of the bacteria pool that cripples some portion of our populace with puzzling regularity. I never get a flu shot because I haven't had the flu for a couple of decades. I've always thought that exposing yourself to the ambient germs of life will go a long way toward making your immune system hardy. If your system has never had to ward off an errant germ, it will be ill-prepared when the oaf across the public transit seat from you sneezes in your face.

Chaos is everywhere.

It's good to take some time, every now and again, to count the many ways we are bestowed good fortune. But having good fortune is scarcely enough. Just as important in this world is what you do with the fortune you are bestowed.

Your fortunes can change, depending on the input you add to the situation. A person who inherits a tremendous amount of money is fortunate. But if a rich person chooses to spend all of their money partying and living the high life, they will likely soon find themselves separated from their money, inside of a body that has been badly abused. Professional athletes and entertainers provide examples of this on a regular basis.

Their gifts of fortune attract the attention of scouts and owners, who are then compelled to provide millions of dollars to secure their talent. But often within several years of retirement, these athletes and entertainers find themselves destitute. How could so much money run through their hands so quickly, we working stiffs ask?

"We make a lot of money, but we spend a lot of money, too," Patrick Ewing of the New York Knicks once said. Apparently, many of them do not spend money on learning how to manage their wealth. Or they trust their money with the wrong wealth managers. Those of us who do not earn as much money in a lifetime as professional athletes make in a single season cannot imagine how they could get themselves into these dilemmas. But life is proportionate. Many of those athletes continue to spend a lot of money even after they stop making a lot of money, and the bank accounts soon run dry.

I am not a deeply religious person, but I have seen enough to believe that, somehow, at the end of the line, each of us shows up at our funeral basically even with the world. Our victories are equally balanced by our defeats. What we stole from the world (and the people within it) is generally equal to what was stolen from us. What we have given is generally equal to what was given to us. "Ashes to ashes, dust to dust," the funeral attendant often quips. In my experience, that is almost always true.

In summary, we are fortunate for the circumstances into which we were born or placed. Perhaps things are more likely to head in one direction or another, based on our fortune, but nearly all of it depends on our actions to bring it to fruition. There are many examples of people who were born into a life of luxury but imploded under the weight of the situation. Likewise, there are people born into no real fortune who forge an impressive life portfolio.

Millions of children per year are born in the United States, just like I was. But many of them will not overcome their situational demons to take advantage of that good fortune. Being fortunate is a good thing, but it is hardly a predictor of success.

Let it be said, however, that it may well be easier to be fortunate if you are born into a pool full of wealth. Your horizons are broader, and there are many more pursuits you need not only dream about, but can actually make come true. Still, we all need the drive and determination to identify and attain our dreams. Much of that comes down to finding the intrinsic value of any given pursuit to your life.

That is sometimes difficult, if you take time to reflect on how important becoming the best figure skater or pool player (or anything else) in the world is, compared to all of the other needs we have in the world. To be fortunate enough to be an expert at anything means that we need to be able to commit significant time to the pursuit. The running theory, as mentioned in Malcolm Gladwell's "The Outliers," is that in order to be an expert at something, we need to do it about 10,000 times. Therefore, in order to perform in an expert fashion over the course of a round of golf, I need to find a way to play about 50,000 hours of golf. A commitment of this sort would, no doubt, have a negative impact on my other desires to be a good husband and father, and a good employee, and a son, and a brother, and a friend to many. But my golf would improve.

Life, perhaps fortunately, always has a way of providing us with options. We all have choices in deciding what we want to be proficient at, what we want to be expert at, and what we just don't have the time to pursue, even though we may have some real talent in a given area.

The Romans allow us to call on the goddess, Fortuna, to grant us a little good fortune at whatever pursuit we are compelled to chase. Of course, it is (according to lore) up to her to grant us the ability to have a positive outcome in a situation that may not warrant such a good result. That may begin to explain how Bob Dylan and Neil Young have continued to be such successful performers for nearly half a century and neither one of them has gotten any better at playing the harmonica or singing. I love them both as musicians, but it isn't because of the precision of their craft. In many ways, it is because of their imprecision. I can play along at home with these artists, and if I squawk an unintended note, I can just bend it into the correct note—like they do.

As mentioned above, fortune is considered a deterministic version of luck. What we were born with was a simple matter of chemistry between our parents. We did not do anything to influence where we landed on this Earth (and what an incredible series of events had to happen for our little life form to be brought to life on this third rock from our Sun), but it is still either fortunate or unfortunate when and where we were born. Assigning the fortune of your circumstances is primarily your own job. We can let other people define our luck as good or bad, but that seems like giving up a lot. It's OK to agree with other people's assessment, but at least forge your own point of view.

Each of us can feel our good or bad fortunes just by looking around. Look at the place where you live. If you live in Indianapolis, you are perhaps disappointed that you don't live in Miami (particularly in the winter). But then again, you don't live in Uganda. There are many great things to relish about any place you happen to have landed. It is human nature to wish for greater fortune, while thanking our lucky stars that it isn't as bad as it could be.

When I travel around the country and introduce myself as being from Nebraska, I detect several different reactions. Some feel a little sorry for the fact that I am so far from the action of the big cities. No oceans, no mountains, and a sometimes-persnickety weather pattern.

On the other hand, I have also disclosed my home state to people who respond with a warm sense of what Nebraska has to offer. The small-town feel, friendly people, shoulder-to-shoulder blue skies, a dark soil that grows its fair share of the food which feeds the world, and the fanaticism of Cornhusker football are often discussed as people recount their experiences with Nebraska. All true.

I believe I have been fortunate to live in the center of the country. With the ocean levels rising, and the intensity of the hurricanes battering the coasts of our continent, I have fewer worries about the future of my house, family and other property. Of course, a tornado can wipe us out next week, but we will likely have plenty of warning and know how to stay out of trouble—although we will stay on the front porch and watch the twister until just after it is safe to do so!

Many of you can rightfully point to the fortune of your birthplace, and the place where you currently live. Neither I nor anyone else can dispute your feelings.

The geography of your existence is only one piece of your prospective fortune. People have described themselves as fortunate for being born into a wealthy family. Others have expressed their gratitude for being born into modest means where a strong work ethic was taught and learned. People have been successful in Sydney, Australia and in Sidney, Nebraska. People can be fortunate (and unfortunate) in both places, and every other place in between.

Who your parents are, and how they are able to mentor your development, is also a point of good and bad fortune. Successful people can generally point to a handful of adults who helped them develop from clueless children into productive citizens. On the other side of life, some of us bear children who serve as guardian angels for us as we age. Life is a fascinating cycle.

Because we need more adults than just our parents to guide us, being assigned a teacher who really connects with students is a fortunate development. Owen Ervin, my high school history teacher and baseball coach, was that person for me. Most of us have a teacher who made a deep impression and shaped our outlook on the world. We usually had no role in determining whether we would be assigned to that teacher's class list. Still, that connection can make all the difference in our fortunes.

Who are the people you feel fortunate to have learned from? Our fortunes may well be gifts from heaven, or they may be the result of a physical force pulsing from above, or they may just be pieces of dumb luck. Historically, we give glory to the gods (in their many forms) for our good fortune—past, present, and future—so that's where we will place it here.

The same fundamental debate can be entertained about many of the physical forces impacting our luck. Let's have a look at some of those.

REFLECTION QUESTIONS

For what things in your life do you feel fortunate?

As you think about it, are there fortunate turns in your life that you take for granted?

Have you been fortunate to find yourself in the company of other fortunate people?

Can we influence our fortune?

CHAPTER 6

PHYSICAL FORCES IMPACTING OUR LUCK

"The pessimist complains about the wind;
The optimist expects it to change;
The realist adjusts the sails."

— William Ward

Golfers and sailors blame the wind. Farmers blame the rain or the barometric pressure. Others have created an art form out of assigning our fates through the positions of the planets and other heavenly bodies. Certainly, some of these elements impact our daily pursuits, but can they sometimes be the difference between success and failure? It makes for good conversation at the coffee shop or around the dinner table to think that any of these forces increases our predisposition toward a certain outcome.

A hearty cottage industry has been created in our society from people who try to explain our likelihood of having a "lucky" or "unlucky" day based on physical forces of nature. In their explanation, they tell us that forces exerted on the Earth by the Moon, the Sun, and all of the planets of our solar system provide us with a unique (at least you and all of the other people in your astrological sign) opportunity to be successful (or not) within a particular area of pursuit.

Several groups are continuing to do research to assert that the weather and the relative exposure to daylight all play a substantial role in the abilities of the human species from day to day. I have always lived in a climate where the sun is visible from the ground about 300 days per year. I have been to places where the sun seemingly never changes the grey view outside the window. I realize I have become accustomed to sunshine. I need to feel the sun on my head and shoulders regularly. If I go for a while without sunshine, it changes my outlook on life (and my ability to detect opportunities for good fortune to find me). Many people living in the higher latitudes find a way to adjust to the irregular solar influence. Some use artificial sun lamps to augment their exposure.

Being alert and aware of your surroundings helps you to identify potential opportunities and mistakes along the way. While some people are ready for the opportunities that come along, others coast naively toward the horizon. Just because you are a Pisces, doesn't mean you will absolutely enjoy a financial windfall today; but if you stay on the lookout for it, the astrologers would suggest, everything is favorable for you to find it.

This explanation of luck attempts to take some of the causation for luck out of our hands. "It just wasn't in the stars," is a common retort. But maybe you just weren't good enough, although that is something we only want to admit as a last resort. I also believe our relative alertness in any situation has some bearing in our ability to react to it.

Maybe your competition was more alert—or just better. But people have always attempted to look for the underlying forces handicapping the human race. In my youth, I always imagined a sort of "situation room" on Mount Olympus, where all of the Gods assembled to monitor our every action on the streets. When someone ran afoul of the Gods' favor, they would invoke their powers of persuasion upon us to rectify the situation. I had clearly envisioned this Supreme Court of our fates, milling about in a sports book setting with big-screen video screens everywhere. Suddenly, the God of the Earth becomes irritated. "If I see one more sin against my word, I am going to make the ground rumble under their feet!"

The God of Wind then becomes irritated about something, somewhere and casts a mighty gust of wind through the town. Fortunately, we have appeased the Gods of Fire by conducting a tremendous bonfire last weekend and praising the powerful and entrancing qualities of the Flame. If we upset the Gods of Earth, Wind, and Fire at the same time, we may find ourselves wishing upon a "Shining Star." Yes, that's a pun. But it's almost that ridiculous to some of us in the 21st century. Still, can you prove there is no basis in fact (at least a little gray area) for these beliefs? Just because you choose to ignore them doesn't mean they don't exist.

If you've ever been to San Francisco or Los Angeles when they haven't been in the throes of a devastating earthquake, you are lucky. Both of those towns have been severely disabled by earthquakes several times over the past century, and they will be again. But if you were there on a warm, sunny day in September . . . Lucky.

After I went to college, my parents moved to the San Francisco Bay Area when my Dad took a job in the mail room at the San Francisco Chronicle. He was driving home from work one sunny early evening in October of 1989 when the Loma Preita earthquake struck and caused the Bay Bridge to collapse. Fortunately for Dad, he had just crossed that bridge about forty-five minutes earlier and was nearly home in Pittsburg when the radio went dead for a few moments. The announcer came back on the air a couple of minutes later to tell listeners a significant earthquake had just struck. Of course, the world would see the event from the pregame coverage of the World Series at Candlestick Park. It is ironic that 1989 was the year Oakland squared off against San Francisco to determine baseball's champion. Maybe the baseball gods were just Angel fans, and wanted to express their displeasure.

If you don't need to personify the force, maybe it is easy to accept that there *are* biorhythms, or an underlying electrical current aiding or impeding our progress on any given day. It is an intriguing theory, which has not yet been either proven or disproven scientifically. Our inability to dismiss its presence makes it a ready receptacle into which we can deposit our success or failures.

Astronomers, looking to the ends of our sight, have identified dark matter as a substance they cannot see, but rather infer its existence by the alteration of light from sources we can see from Earth. According to Wikipedia, which may not offer the most scientific explanation, but perhaps more useful to us of more Earth-bound minds:

*"**Dark matter** is a type of matter hypothesized in astronomy and cosmology to account for effects that appear to be the result of mass where no such mass can be seen. Dark matter cannot be seen directly with telescopes; evidently it neither emits nor absorbs light or other electromagnetic radiation at any significant level. It is otherwise hypothesized to simply be matter that is not reactant to light.[1] Instead, the existence and properties of dark matter are inferred from its gravitational effects on visible matter, radiation, and the large-scale structure of the universe. According to the Planck mission team, and based on the standard model of cosmology, the total mass–energy of the known universe contains 4.9% ordinary matter, 26.8% dark matter and 68.3% dark energy. Thus, dark matter is estimated to constitute 84.5% of the total matter in the universe, while dark energy plus dark matter constitute 95.1% of the total content of the universe."*

The preceding text is taken from Wikipedia Encyclopedia
http://en.wikipedia.org/wiki/Dark_matter

1.   **Trimble, V.** (1987). "Existence and nature of dark matter in the universe". *Annual Review of Astronomy and Astrophysics* **25**:   425–472.   Bibcode:1987ARA&A..25..425T. doi:10.1146/annurev.aa.25.090187.002233.

2.   **Ade, P. A. R.; Aghanim, N.; Armitage-Caplan, C.**; *et al.* (Planck Collaboration) (22 March 2013). "Planck 2013 results. I. Overview of products and scientific results—Table 9". *Astronomy and Astrophysics* **1303**: 5062. arXiv:1303.5062. Bibcode:2013arXiv1303.5062P.

3.   **Francis, Matthew** (22 March 2013). "First Planck results: the Universe is still weird and interesting". *Arstechnica.*

4. "Planck captures portrait of the young Universe, revealing earliest light". University of Cambridge. 21 March 2013. Retrieved 21 March 2013.

5. **Sean Carroll, Ph.D.**, Cal Tech, 2007, The Teaching Company, *Dark Matter, Dark Energy: The Dark Side of the Universe*, Guidebook Part 2 page 46, Accessed Oct. 7, 2013, "...dark matter: An invisible, essentially collisionless component of matter that makes up about 25 percent of the energy density of the universe... it's a different kind of particle... something not yet observed in the laboratory..."

Dark matter, thus far, has gone relatively undetected until recently, and thus we know almost nothing about it. If dark matter and energy comprise 95 percent of the universe, though, isn't it reasonable to think some traces of it might be lurking in our atmosphere, impacting our daily results.

Can you maintain your belief in God, and believe these (dark and otherwise) forces *do* play a role in our daily fate? With a Creator so thorough in His accounting of our actions, how could you dismiss the possibility that He created all of these forces for us to use as a guide during our life on Earth?

There have been many belief systems developed by humanity to explain the world around us. Medicine men, voodoo doctors, and the traveling evangelical road shows have all promised us better fates. The following chapters discuss some of the more prevalent practices we use in our modern lives in an effort to improve (or anticipate) our fates.

ASTROLOGY AND ITS
ROLE IN OUR FATES

"About astrology and palmistry: they are good because they make people vivid and full of possibilities. They are communism at its best. Everybody has a birthday and almost everybody has a palm."

— Kurt Vonnegut

Every morning, thousands of people still riffle through the morning paper. More and more, in the first half of the 21ˢᵗ century, people have surrendered the hard copy for the electronic news fix in the morning. No matter your method of ingesting the information, however, there is always an opportunity for readers to get a daily horoscope prognostication. It is comforting to many of us to get a glimpse of our daily predisposition for success or failure.

I have noticed that people always get a little more out of the horoscope when they read it at the end of the day. This way, we can mold the events of the day into the cryptic messages provided for the people under our sign.

Just try to research the history of horoscopes online, and you will avail yourself of an array of opinions about how your day will be.

Many people have made a career out of bringing the art of the public horoscope reading. Evangeline Adams, Marguerite Carter, Linda Black, Liz Greene, Julia Parker, Jackie Stallone (yes, Sylvester's mother), Sydney Omarr, Roger Elliott and Frederick Davies all made names for themselves using the news publications to give people a personal stake in the medium of astrology.

Horoscopes have been packaged as a wonderful feature throughout the history of the news business. Jeanne Dixon made a career out of it, claiming her start when a gypsy came through her town, gave her a crystal, and read her palm. The palm reading indicated that she would be a seer and would advise many important people. What better certification could you need to be a real star in the business?

Apparently none, because she went on to syndicate her horoscope column to hundreds of newspapers across the globe. She ended up providing horoscopic advice to both Presidents Nixon and Reagan. Knowing the generally accepted consequences for the Moon, or Jupiter or Venus being in play for each sign group is the loose science surrounding this discipline, but does the physical universe (and particularly our solar system) really have an impact on how likely we are to be lucky today?

The point is, many people have made a habit out of the horoscope. Many others have made a living. The phrases, admonitions, and encouragements are offered each day, with one being applicable to each of us. Some columns come with a number assigned to denote what today's relative outlook will be on a scale of one to ten. Some of us take these things with a grain of salt, while others may assign a little more credibility to it, especially if we are reading it one day later and something ended up making sense, in retrospect.

Horoscope writers are careful to stand atop the fence. While, according to the planetary alignment, "you may find trouble with your finances today," using "a penny saved is a penny earned," is another way to communicate the sentiment to hold on to your money for another day. You will never see an astrological prediction that suggests "you should bet it all on a hunch." That contains a little too much liability.

To get everything on the table I should admit, at one time in my journalistic career, I authored the horoscope. It was a spur-of-the-moment idea in the newsroom of the Aspen Daily News where the idea for a column was born. Many crazy ideas came up in this three-person workspace. Many of the ideas died on the vine after we got to the part of the discussion where we asked, "So who's going to *do* this?" Somehow, this opportunity leaped out and grabbed me. So I volunteered. Sure, I could have some fun with it.

I cannot claim to have any mystical connections with the heavens, or the experience of having any traveling gypsies handing out crystals. Instead, I used my creative mind and a deft ability to access double-entendre, and launched out on a foray into the cosmos as the seer, "Ursa Majors." Twelve brief quips aimed at providing a smile to those who were looking for one, and probably, some life guidance to those who created a habit out of the horoscope.

It was an admittedly irreverent move by a 25-year-old wet-behind-the-ears journalist into the world of mystic force and folly. And yet many people who knew no better, took the words that appeared under their star sign, and tried to apply it to what was happening in their lives. Fewer people did the same with any of my news reports from the city council or school board meetings.

Initially, I tried to research horoscope writing, to see if there was any process or formula. Where do I tap into the mystic river? Soon I realized that no major university offers a degree in astrology. It was a niche profession, thinly shrouded in the supernatural. Applying the position of the celestial bodies into the context of our lives is something our society has given credence to, along with palm readers and crystal ball gazers. All you really need is the feeling that you have a "sixth sense" (or be able to sell your mysticism to others) along with a flair for writing, and you are off and running . . . unless you happen upon a gypsy passing through town.

In my somewhat brief career as a horoscopic mystic, I mostly twisted popular sayings and music lyrics into a series of encouragements, warnings and admonitions. Our reactions to the events of the day are, of course, the surest indicator of good or bad fortune. My quips of written art might easily have fit into the events of your life, but not based on the pull of your Moon.

My own folly in the world of horoscopic writing aside, there *are* days when it's just easier to be successful. Why is this true? The answer, of course, is different for each of us, and therefore difficult to universally define for all of us. Even breaking us down into twelve different star signs doesn't allow for much delineation between our vastly different life results.

Interestingly, it seems that while astrologers are searching for ways to explain luck, they do not generally believe that it is a haphazard and random phenomenon. Rather, they see our fates as they follow "identifiable" patterns and principles of life (including the gravitational pulls of Uranus).

So while they pledge allegiance to the physical forces and properties to give their predictions credence, they must also provide an array of caveats, which you can hear from most astrologers, which go something like this:

"Astrology may be able to predict whether you are going to have a good few years in the near future or go through a rough time, but it may not be able to predict the reasons for it. Astrological predictions are all made, keeping in mind, that things will run their natural course. But due to variables such as the Free Will of people, such events may not always come to pass in their natural course and may be affected by the choices

that any person makes at any point in their life. These choices, which are made out of your Free Will, can alter predictions about the future, positively as well as negatively.

Thus, although the cosmic bodies and their positions are a very accurate and reliable source of knowing the future, what is also true is that no one is bound by the stars, and all of us make choices which affect our future and the astrological predictions about it."

So, while the physical forces of the universe are predictable, individuals have the power to upset the cosmos and go against the grain. So we have what would be categorized as a "dark art" clinging to science as its basis, as long as humans don't sabotage it by being human. It's sounding easier to just have the gypsy come through town and bestow me with the "mystical sense."

As flippant as I may appear, I cannot dismiss the influence the planets and the Moon may have on the relative enjoyability of our lives on a given day. The forces may even be powerful enough to dictate whether we are fully prepared to face all of the opportunities coming our way.

There are, of course, people who hear all of this talk about whether we are going to have a good day or a bad day, and pass it off as drivel. They are dispassionately consumed by the notion that someday, all of this will be rendered useless by the next big meteorite aimed at this little planet we call home. What difference is today's fortune if there is a giant trump card waiting in space to plummet us into rubble? Many previous meteorite impacts on Earth have demonstrated the climate-changing capabilities of such an event, but worrying about that eventuality is a terrible way to go through life.

We are here, now. We have really beaten the odds to get to where we are. Aren't we kind of playing with the "house's money" in this life?

From our selfish, human perspective, any future asteroid collision with Earth will be completely random. But can we say that it is not all part of God's plan? Absent the horror of Armageddon, how much of our relative fortuity can we credit to the heavens? Conversely, how much of our end result is to our own credit or fault? How much is just a matter of fate?

I know many teachers (and cops) who would testify to the existence of a "full moon" effect, when it comes to the anxiety levels students bring into their classrooms (and citizens to their everyday interpersonal interactions). Maybe this is just a visible example of the influences atmospheric and extraterrestrial forces can have on our bodies.

Some of us may be able to muscle through the physical forces limiting us, but if you aren't determined to persevere, mightn't a percentage of the Capricorns be unable to grasp an important concept today? Of course, a control group is now difficult to assemble because many of us have already seen the forecast for today's events, and depending on its tenor, we may believe we are destined to succeed in a particular area—or to fail. Or we may become determined to prove the horoscope is wrong today, doing everything in our power to run counter to the predicted pull of the cosmic forces.

Again, astrological readings try to offer us a predisposition to have a good or a bad day, even before luck arrives on the scene. Just because you lose the coin flip, it doesn't really mean the forces are out to keep you from winning. Maybe you are better positioned to play a reactionary game, instead of initiating the action.

The first unfortunate turn of events does not necessarily dictate the ultimate outcome. Perhaps the influence of Mars could not anticipate the errant bounce that botches your first opportunity. But if the planets really are pulling your direction, perhaps the next opportunity will be the beginning of a series of positive developments, as long as you don't allow yourself to anticipate further misfortune.

REFLECTION QUESTIONS

How often do you check your horoscope?

If you believe in the extra-terrestrial forces at play, how deeply do you believe these cosmic forces impact the results of our lives?

Have you chosen love interests based on an astrological sign?

SUPERSTITIONS

"Depend on the rabbit's foot if you will, but remember it didn't work for the rabbit."

— R. E. Shay

The history of superstitions spans mankind's existence. Humans have always wanted to believe a certain set of actions, or an inanimate object, is charged with fateful energy that will either bring a desired result to pass, or prevent the undesirable from occurring.

Coining the phenomenon as "superstition" came in the wake of the vast popularity of crediting (or blaming) life's results on an array of "godly" influences.

The term superstition was first recorded by Greek and Roman polytheists, who scorned the people who constantly trembled with fear at the thought of the gods, as a slave feared a cruel and capricious master. Such fear of the gods was what the Romans meant by "superstition."

(Histoire de la vie privée, vol. I, Le Seuil, 1987, p. 211)

In modern day society, superstitions are little things that people work into their daily habits in hopes that it will bring them good luck (or help them avoid bad luck). The origin of this lucky force is never completely known and rarely questioned. The acts have just become part of the cultural norm, and you can choose those with which you can most relate.

Our friends at Merriam Webster dictionary harshly describe superstition as "a belief or way of behaving that is based on fear of the unknown and faith in magic" or even a "false conception of causation." They suggest that superstitions are performed in an effort to influence supernatural, natural, or Godly forces that might be at play in our lives.

su·per·sti·tion (from Merriam Webster's online dictionary)

> *1a : a belief or practice resulting from ignorance, fear of the unknown, trust in magic or chance, or a false conception of causation;*
> *b : an irrational abject attitude of mind toward the supernatural, nature, or God resulting from superstition*
> *2 : a notion maintained despite evidence to the contrary*

"By permission. From *Merriam-Webster's Collegiate® Dictionary, 11th Edition* ©2014 by Merriam-Webster, Inc. (www.Merriam-Webster.com)."

I think people in the 21st century are more likely to participate in superstitions just to have a "stake in the game" of life. It is a faint opportunity to influence our fate that just might overcome any situation with which we are faced. Knock on wood.

From its first use in the Classical Latin of Livy and Ovid (1st century BC), the term "superstitio" is used in the pejorative sense it still holds today, of an excessive fear of the gods or unreasonable religious belief, as opposed to *religio*, the proper, reasonable awe of the gods. While many definitions attempt to position superstition as the exact opposite of religion, there are some who would say that highly religious people are doing little more than drawing on their superstitions. Praying at certain times of the day and night, crossing yourself, and even taking communion could be nothing more than ritualistic superstition, if it turns out in the end that there is no Higher Being.

In 1520, Martin Luther called the papacy, "that fountain and source of all superstitions." Thus these correlations have been suggested for many years. Whether it is or not, of course, continues to be debated.

Superstitions are probably the least scientific of our cause-and-effect study of luck and fortune, but it may be the most practiced. In fact, superstitions are one of the most likely things parents will pass on to their children, giving the practice some credence until such time that it is proven invalid—which is difficult to do.

Scientists, such as B.F. Skinner in 1948, project that the proliferation of superstitions may be no more than simple-minded humans trying to realize good fortune through a series of events, and then when similar results are desired, similar rituals are undertaken.

Skinner's research was conducted initially on pigeons, where certain actions delivered food. But even after the food stopped coming, the pigeons continued their actions that earlier delivered the food. It was a true study in reinforcement behaviors that, for the pigeons, might no longer deliver the food for a thousand cycles, but what if it started again? When the cause-and-effect relationship is removed, the action almost becomes a ritualistic imperative, even if it is no longer productive.

The syndrome Skinner first identified in the pigeons is now described as the *partial reinforcement effect*, and this has been used to explain superstitious behavior in humans. To be more precise, this effect means that, whenever an individual performs an action expecting reinforcement, and none seems forthcoming, it actually creates a sense of persistence within the individual.

Other researchers have taken this study further, suggesting that the partial reinforcement effect strongly parallels superstitious behavior in humans because the individuals feel that, by continuing this action, reinforcement will happen. Or individuals believe that reinforcement has come at certain times in the past as a result of this action, although not all the time, and this may be one of those effective times.

I know that sounds pretty clinical, but I recall having a conversation much like that with myself on more than one occasion. "What if I don't wear this lucky jersey and my favorite team loses?"

It reminds me a little bit of the old days of television (before cable and satellite technology), when a "snowy" picture on the television screen could often be resolved by laying one hand on the console and the other hand pointing into the air in the general direction of the TV station's transmission tower, as if to create an antenna out of yourself. Others merely rapped on the side of the television. Occasionally, the picture would improve. Whether it helped or not, it could never be proven, but it never seemed to take long after the picture faded to a scratchy mess in our family's living room for someone to give it a try.

Superstitions may just make us feel like we are doing something to alter the foreboding outcomes of our lives. There is usually no physical reason why finding a penny face up brings good luck and allows you to do better on your math exam. Similarly, the black cat, whose path you crossed on the way to class, really has no idea what you are going to face today. Good omens, such as the lucky penny, might just serve as an encouraging sign that your culture sees to be good luck, which in turn improves your confidence about your ability to do well in an upcoming challenge.

As absurd as some of it is, there is no shortage of people practicing superstitions from the following list (and more). The list below only covers a portion of the superstitions with which I have come into contact. There are others coming to my attention almost weekly. The number of lucky socks, lucky underwear, and lucky hats cannot be reasonably calculated throughout the world. And it's not wise to doubt the prospective good luck that may be coming your way. Personal doubt only clouds the ability of the lucky forces to work on you, and allows the evil forces to prevail. If you have a role in making your own luck, it pays to stay optimistic about such things, just in case it does make a difference.

Here is a list of a few superstitions with which I became familiar during my upbringing:

- A rabbit's foot brings good luck;
- If you are talking about your good luck thus far, knock on wood to help your good luck continue;
- An apple a day keeps the doctor away;
- To find a four-leaf clover is to find good luck;
- If you walk under a ladder, you will have bad luck;
- If a black cat crosses your path, you will have bad luck;
- To break a mirror will bring you seven years bad luck;
- To open an umbrella in the house is to bring bad luck;
- To find (or touch) a horseshoe brings good luck;
- Step on a crack, break your mother's back;
- Crossing your fingers is a common plea for good luck;

- Gamblers often blow on the dice for good luck before tossing them;
- You can break a bad luck spell by turning seven times in a clockwise circle;
- Garlic protects people from evil spirits and vampires;
- At the end of a rainbow is a pot of gold;
- Clothes worn inside out will bring good luck;
- Wearing your birthstone will bring you good luck;
- If you blow out all of the candles on your birthday cake with the first breath, you will get whatever you wish for;
- To have a wish come true using a wishbone, two people make a wish, then take hold of each end of the bone and pull it until it separates. The person with the longer end gets his or her wish;
- An itchy palm means money will come your way;
- Eating fish makes you smart;
- Toads cause warts;
- A cricket in the house brings good luck;
- The appearance of a ladybug is seen as good luck;
- Crossing your fingers helps to avoid bad luck and helps a wish come true;
- It is bad luck to sing at the table;
- It is bad luck to sleep on a table;
- After receiving a container of food, the container should never be returned empty;
- A lock of hair from a baby's first haircut should be kept for good luck;
- A bird that comes in your window brings bad luck;
- To refuse a kiss under mistletoe causes bad luck;
- Goldfish in the pond brings good luck;
- Goldfish in the house brings bad luck;

- For good luck, wear new clothes on Easter;
- An acorn at the window can keep lightning out of the house;
- If the bottom of your feet itch, you will make a trip;
- If your palms itch, you are about to experience good luck;
- When a dog howls, death is near;
- It is bad luck to chase someone with a broom;
- A sailor wearing an earring cannot drown;
- To find a penny heads up, brings good luck;
- To drop a dishcloth means bad luck is coming;
- If you shiver, someone is casting a shadow on your grave;
- To make a happy marriage, the bride must wear: something old, something new, something borrowed, something blue;
- The wedding veil protects the bride from the evil eye;
- It is bad luck for the groom to lay eyes on his bride on the day leading up to the wedding;
- Washing a car will bring rain;
- You must get out of bed on the same side you got in on or you will have bad luck;
- Evil spirits cannot harm you when you are standing in a circle;
- It is unlucky to rock an empty rocking chair;
- To kill an albatross is to cause bad luck to the ship and all upon it;
- Wearing an opal when it is not your birthstone is bad luck;
- Spilling salt has historically been associated with bad luck;
- Tossing some salt over your shoulder, particularly after spilling it, is seen as good luck;

- To give someone a purse or wallet without money in it will bring that person bad luck;

Growing up in the 20th century America, a person was apt to run across more than a handful of these superstitions. Many people asked questions about the acts, particularly the first time they came across them. But even without much thoughtful reasoning behind them, the superstitions take flight and perpetuate. In many cases, the superstition becomes a common ritual in the relationship between two people. If two people can understand what is meant when a friend knocks on wood, or urges them to "break a leg," there is a special understanding, even if the desired outcome doesn't result.

I am sure there are other superstitions you have witnessed that are not on the list. If you don't really require a visible cause-and-effect link between one thing and another, it opens up a world of possibilities larger than any book about superstitions could contain.

Superstitions live on because they have been passed on from one generation to the next. Even today, where direct evidence and facts outweigh superstitious beliefs, there are very few of us who can deny that we do not at least secretly harbor a warm spot in our brains for one or two superstitions. The feeling is universal. We don't know with any certainty whether superstition works, but we dare not test fate (and fly in the face of societal norms) by ignoring it.

Many superstitions were simply made up, and many more have certainly been perpetuated through the media over the years. As a recent Friday the 13th approached, there were mentions of the prospective bad luck by numerous news anchors attempting to make mindless banter in an effort to demonstrate their "human side."

Doctors' offices make appointments on Friday the 13th and always pause for just an instant. "We'll hope that date is just a coincidence," they say with a nervous laugh, not knowing how much credence the person on the other end of the line might give to the connection between the date and their fate.

Weddings are filled with superstitions, although the institution of marriage has not benefitted much from all of it. From the preparation (something old, something new . . .), to carrying the bride across the threshold, there are forces at play throughout the process. Even the throwing of rice (or birdseed, as we wedding-goers evolve into the 21st century) at the couple as they exit the church is said to transfer the Earth's fertility to the couple.

As a reflection of our culture of the time, Hollywood has given life to these beliefs many times. "Every time you hear a bell ring, an angel gets his wings." "I'm looking over a four-leaf clover, that I overlooked before . . ." The culture of superstition perpetuates, and Hollywood has the power to give it wings by re-writing the endings.

Maybe superstitions just provide us with a way to have a stake in the game of life. If the true outcome of a situation is mostly out of our control, at least by wearing a pair of lucky socks, we can try to persuade the forces-that-be to treat us favorably. Does wearing the jersey of your favorite team really help them to succeed in any larger measure during the game? For those of you with more than one piece of team gear, does the particular lucky shirt you wore when the team won the Super Bowl *really* help them to perform better? In a big game, though, you will still search for *that* shirt, won't you?

Yup, me too.

Throughout my life, I have gotten closest to the world of superstition during my time in competitive sports. Athletes are notorious for their sometimes-outrageous superstitions. Same meal, arrive at the park at the same time, with the same sequence of putting the uniform on, going through the warm-up cycle in exactly the same way every day. Have you ever watched how many times any one of a number of baseball players will secure and unsecure the Velcro wristband on their batting gloves when they are up to bat? Nomar Garciaparra was the first player I noticed with this annoying ritual, but many others have found comfort in it. If they didn't think it helped them, I'm sure they wouldn't do it. The batting glove adjustment is almost more pervasive than the players who cross themselves (or pull on the shoulder of their jerseys, or tap home plate with their bat, or any one of a dozen other rituals) before they get into the batter's box. These rituals become a very real part of a player's "getting ready sequence." For many players, the mechanical sequence of events begins when they are in the on-deck circle, or even before the game starts. Many players have maintained the same ritual for many years, and for those who have ascended to the highest level of professional baseball, why mess with a good thing?

You'll notice as we get to the playoffs of any men's sport, fewer and fewer players will shave until the playoff run is completed. As unsightly as this becomes over time, it is considered unlucky to shave during the playoffs by many players. That superstition is mostly responsible for why World Series locker room interviews look more like a mountain man rendezvous with all of the four- and five-week beards running around the clubhouse. I want to see Bob Costas doing an interview in the winner's locker room that starts something like this: "We'd like to get Jeremiah Johnson over here for just a moment to get his comments."

Wade Boggs, who was inducted into the Baseball Hall of Fame in 2005, had a very specific regimen that included eating chicken prior to each game. We'll never know whether he would have achieved as much without his chicken dinners, but there are many people who are happy he found something which gave him the confidence and nutrition to be successful.

Even the socially acceptable act of wishing God's blessings on someone who sneezes is rooted in superstition. This superstition developed out of early man's belief that his breath was representative of his soul. It was believed, at one point in human history, your soul could escape swiftly in the course of a violent sneeze. Conversely, it has been said that the devil can enter your body during a sneeze. But having someone say "God bless you" immediately following your sneeze is supposed to drive the devil away.

Pope Gregory the Great decreed, in the throes of the Plague in sixth-century Europe, that a prayer be said over anyone who sneezed, since sneezing was one of the fatal symptoms of the disease. When the Black Plague returned in the 15th century, the papacy again declared that anyone who sneezed must be blessed, as the person's death was imminent.

Even though the art of sneezing continues, and it is still a pretty effective method of spewing disease to anyone else in your airspace, the direct correlation with death has been mostly eliminated. Still, though, you will find people yelling "bless you" down the hallway to cover the exposed soul of a colleague at work.

From a strictly scientific level, it seems rather silly. But none of us can prove this relationship between sneezes and spirits totally wrong, and it seems like such a small gesture (that has been wrapped in the sense of kindly caring for the well-being of others) so, God bless you!

Sneezing is one of the body's mechanism used to internally "shift gears." As we recover from the sneeze, and before we take our foot off the clutch to return to our life at hand, there is an instant in which we can ground ourselves in the good wishes of our friends and co-workers.

The beauty of the "God bless you" greeting, as I plan to deliver it henceforth, is not to chase away the evil spirits. Instead, it is my understanding that God's blessings are present for all to find. It is up to you to decide how you will feel blessed by God today. I am merely wishing you an encouragement to find your blessing(s). Even if today's blessing seems more like a consolation prize than the major blessing you were hoping to receive, the blessing is there for you every day, somewhere. I hope you can find it.

God bless you! After all, there isn't enough kindly hope being shared for our fellow man in the world today.

REFLECTION QUESTIONS

What superstitions do you regularly observe?

Which do you think are absurd and useless?

What makes the superstitions you don't practice less valid than the ones you believe in?

Do you practice superstitions handed down from your elders?

"Weather"
We Are Lucky or Not

"Good luck has its storms."

— George Lucas

With the dilution of the media segregating our society's common knowledge, the weather is perhaps the last real common experience people in a community have with each other. Your friend on the north end of town got a quarter-inch of rain last night, while no rain fell at your house. In the middle of a dry, hot summer, he (and his lawn) is right to feel very lucky.

For me, November and February are really depressing months. In November, the fall is slowly fading into the imprisonment of winter. The transition creates incessantly gray skies, and the days become noticeably shorter. This is the time of year in the middle latitudes of the northern hemisphere where we begin to go to work in the dark, and return home in the dark. Many of our dispositions also begin to go dark. Most of us can endure short periods of this torture, but November is the beginning of nearly three months of only watching the sunlight through the office window.

February sits at the opposite bookend of the winter season. The anticipation for the spring warm-up is well underway, but the Earth takes its time bringing its wave of warmth to bear. I usually spend some portion of the month recovering from a respiratory illness, so it is small comfort to me that February is the shortest month of the year.

At any time of the year, the weather can create anxiety, and sometimes an accompanying inability to be at our best. You are free to harbor your own feelings toward the weather patterns where you live.

School teachers across this country will tell you they have their own little barometers sitting at the desks in their classrooms. When the weather is about to change, students have a little harder time sitting in their seats. Maintaining the decorum necessary to line up and walk in an orderly fashion to the cafeteria or to the music room becomes more difficult.

For children who are overly energetic every day, the intensity rises beyond controllable levels when a storm front is approaching. We can all feel the changes when we stand outside an hour or two before a storm hits. There seems to be more friction in the air.

Perhaps it is the air masses colliding, rubbing particles together and charging the atmosphere. Sometimes you can even witness the hair on your arms standing at attention, signaling that friction in the air—and in the minds of those of us breathing that air.

For many people, an aching knee or shoulder foretells a change in the weather, in addition to providing them with a more challenging task in performing life's day-to-day functions.

Farmers can tell you when unsettled weather is moving in. The animals get edgy, almost spooked. We used to have a dog that, I swear, could sense thunder and lightning from fifty miles away. Barkley used to begin whimpering and whining when the skies were still blue overhead. He would quickly change from a dog with boundless energy, to a cowering puppy. When the first cloud began to show itself on the horizon, he would seek out the darkest, most secluded shelter he could find. We would often find him trembling behind the workbench in the garage. When he saw an opportunity to get into the house, he made a beeline. My best guess is that Barkley could feel the rumbling of the Earth through his paws. Many pet owners report the same sorts of reactions in earthquake country.

Those of us who wear shoes are sometimes insulated from the vibrations of the world around us.

In the Great Plains of the United States, where tremendous thunderstorms are born and raised, we can sense the static electricity in the air, and the mixing of air masses well in advance of the rain and lightning's arrival. This is true, in some measure, because weather fronts bring with them changes in wind direction and dramatic dips in the barometric pressure.

Also, no matter where you live, the prevailing wind direction can have a significant effect on the weather. In the center of the North American continent, winds from the north come from the Arctic regions. Southern winds blow up from Mexico. West winds originate from the Pacific, after making it over the Rocky Mountains. Today's weather, and some of our predisposition about the day's events, is significantly impacted by which direction the wind is blowing.

No matter the temperature, don't you find the world to be just a little more serene when the winds are calm? Rain and snow do not scramble my ability to concentrate more than a twenty or thirty mile per hour wind whistling through my ears. It just seems to scramble my ions. Be it the serenity of the neighborhood after a winter's snowfall, or a wonderful early summer evening on the deck, having the wind stand at ease creates a little bit of what we hope Heaven to be.

What's more, depending on the Sun's position in relation to where you live, you may also be suffering from Seasonal Affective Disorder, a mood disorder associated with depression episodes and related to seasonal variations of light. In its more serious form, it is characterized by "depressed affect, lethargy, loss of libido, hypersomnia, excessive weight gain, carbohydrate cravings, anxiety and inability to concentrate or focus during the late autumn or winter" (Nelson 1990).

Nelson, Badura, Goldman. Mechanisms of Seasonal Cycles of Behavior. Annual Review of Psychology. 1990. 41: 81-108.

Can it be just a sad coincidence that depression and even suicide attempts increase during the time of the year when the sun is least prevalent in our lives?

"[...P]leasant weather (higher temperature or barometric pressure) was related to higher mood, better memory, and "broadened" cognitive style during the spring as time spent outside increased. The same relationships between mood and weather were not observed during other times of year, and indeed hotter weather was associated with lower mood in the summer.

"These results are consistent with findings on seasonal affective disorder, and suggest that pleasant weather improves mood and broadens cognition in the spring because people have been deprived of such weather during the winter."

Keller, Matthew C.; Fredrickson, Barbara L.; Ybarra, Oscar; Côté, Stéphane; Johnson, Kareem; Mikels, Joe; Conway, Anne; Wager, Tor; (2005). A Warm Heart and a Clear Head: The Contingent Effects of Weather on Mood and Cognition. Psychological Science, 16(9), 724-731.

Our reaction to the lack of sunlight seems like a no-brainer in Alaska or other higher latitudes, but even in the central or southern United

States, there is a very discernible difference in the amount of sunlight available in June versus December.

Thus, if we buy into the notion that our outlook and disposition have an impact on the luck and good fortune people experience throughout the day, isn't it wise to take the weather into account? Or is it merely creating a self-fulfilling prophecy? Perhaps it doesn't affect our luck as much as simply providing us a predisposition for how we think our day is going to go—and then whatever happens for the positive during our day just makes our dreams come true.

In parts of the world where agricultural production is a way of life, there are always people talking about good luck or bad luck when it comes to the weather. Do the winds and rains come at the right time? If you are growing corn, there is a tenuous time when the corn grows tall enough that it cannot support its full weight if a strong wind comes along. Once it matures a little further, its root system strengthens and, standing next to thousands of its fellow corn stalks, it can endure stronger winds. Hail can always come forth and strip the plants of their potential harvest. An early freeze can also create a negative impact on a farmer's crop.

Farming is, in fact, the ultimate test of luck. No matter your crop, there are always conditions which can twist the best practices (and the best of the farmer's intentions) into nothing more than a pile of silage. While science has disproven some of the popular superstitions of farming (planting dates have gotten much earlier with advancements in seed technology), there are still superstitions or rituals used to determine when the best time to plant or harvest might be. Planting and harvest are, after all, the only two times farmers truly have a majority of the control. Once 500 acres of ground is planted with seed, it becomes a stationary target upon which the weather Gods may take aim.

"When you first hear the locusts, it will be six weeks until the first frost."

"Rain never comes up for a full moon."

"In the fall, a frost is most likely during a full moon."

While people who grow their income outdoors are always talking about the luck of the weather and the elements, there are precious few things they can do to change the facts. When you plant, and in what configuration, is constantly debated. But these decisions are made based on the most likely scenarios and occurrences. Over the years, many in the farm community have relied on the Farmer's Almanac for guidance. Will this be an early spring or a late winter? When will the first frost arrive? Will the rains come early or late this year, or will they come at all? There are many theories on the subject. Some include watching how the wildlife is behaving. Others live by the axiom that the coldest nights of the month generally occur around the full moon.

Planting of lines of trees to serve as wind breaks has been a tremendous benefit to farmers across the open prairies. Planting windbreaks and changing the tilling practices after the harvest, are among the lessons learned from the Dust Bowl years of the 1930s. Mother Nature, though, can still be unpredictable and bring a storm from an unusual direction, and at unusual points in the growing season.

While it is frequently characterized as luck, most of the twists and turns in a farmer's life are better described as good (and bad) fortune. Maybe it's even dumb luck. Across the vast open plains, a hail storm can blow through and create a mile-wide swath of destruction, while farmers outside the hail cloud merely enjoy some much-needed summer rain.

Looking at the devastation of their neighbors, they can feel infinitely fortunate for their geographic placement in relation to that particular storm, but they can take no comfort in their location when the next dark cloud comes over the horizon.

Over time, as we chart the track of storms over the years, we can perhaps get a better idea about preferred paths for storms. We might be able to identify certain areas that are more likely to be hit with a tornado-laden hailstorm than others, once we look at data from the past 100 years. We have identified a pattern with the drought cycle (which some say are related to sunspots and solar flare patterns), which encourages us to plant drought-resistant crops during the anticipated dry years. Certainly, people with land located in a river valley can expect to be flooded more often than those with land on top of the hill. But the severe winds will be more devastating to the hill-toppers.

Life on the farm is nothing, if not a game of chance. Even if you manage to sidestep the destruction from the weather, then you have to hope this isn't the year the grasshoppers (or some other insect) decide to descend over the crops in your area.

Veteran grain farmer Ken Miller told me that, more than superstitions, farmers will mimic their neighbors. "If my neighbor is irrigating (or spraying for weeds or insects), I start to think he must know something I don't, so I will do what he is doing."

Sometimes the power of superstition extends no further than your line of sight.

I admire farmers for their dogged determination to deliver a crop through all of the potential complications. It is amazing that the United States is still able to feed most of the world with its harvest. But it takes someone with a special relationship with the elements to be able to stomach the uncertainty farming demands. In short, every successful farmer needs a good deal of luck. It is just unclear, year to year, what kind of luck they will need.

Farmers often find themselves quietly hoping for a reduction in yield in other areas of the country. For example, the fortunes of Nebraska farmers rise a little when Illinois or Iowa is stuck in a drought pattern, or has recurrent spates of hail. Less corn from the most prolific corn-growing states generally increases the price of each bushel. If everyone has a great year, the market glut will drive down the prices. This can result in a record harvest with only a mediocre financial benefit.

It is usually not until after the season is over that a farmer knows what kind of luck he (or she) had. On the other hand, isn't that the way luck usually happens for all of us?

Certainly, the weather is not the ultimate predictor of how the chips will fall for us on a given day. But depending on the reaction we humans bring to the occasion, we can put ourselves at either an advantage or a disadvantage before luck ever comes into play.

REFLECTION QUESTIONS

How does the weather affect you?

Does it impact your ability to be successful on a given day?

Do you see changes in other drivers or customers as the weather changes?

Is There Something in a Number?

"This is the third time; I hope good luck lies in odd numbers.... There is divinity in odd numbers, either in nativity, chance, or death."

— William Shakespeare

Throughout human history, many cultures have attempted to unlock the code to their fates using numbers. The Chinese, Japanese, Greek, Hebrews, Egyptians, Phoenicians, early Christians, Mayans and Incas all employed number systems in an attempt to gain a deeper understanding of themselves and the universe.

The western form of Numerology, the Pythagorean system, has evolved as the most enduring and popular of all numerological systems ever created. Pythagorean Numerology was organized by Greek philosopher and mathematician Pythagoras, who combined the mathematical disciplines of the Arabic, Druid, Phoenician, Egyptian and Essene sciences. As it evolved, it was incorporated as the spiritual basis for many secret societies, such as the Rosicrusians, Masons, Anthroposophists and others.

Hans Decoz, who has authored a book and appears regularly online, notes that Numerology columns now appear regularly in newspapers and magazines, as people look for guidance from the "science of the numbers."

"Numerologists are consulted with increasing regularity for everything from personal romance to business decisions. As the industrialized world becomes more computerized and dependent on numerical systems, the fascination with this ancient spiritual science only grows."

Excerpted from Numerologist Hans Decoz's book *"Numerology: Key to Your Inner Self"*

For a variety of reasons, and with a variety of justifications, most cultures have developed a system whereby we consider some numbers to be lucky or unlucky. Even if you don't subscribe to all the common American folklore about "lucky number 7," you probably have some number between 1 and 10 that you choose regularly, if pressed.

The practice of Pythagorean numerology assigns certain characteristics and traits to each of the numbers 1 through 9, as well as 11 and 22. Then it creates a process by which you use your date of birth, or your given name, to calculate a number by which your demeanor is determined. Depending on how I add all of that up, I am an 11 (or a 2). The complicated formula for determining "your number" can be found at http://www.wikihow.com/Calculate-Your-Name-Number-in-Numerology.

Being relatively unaware of this formal system of determining a lucky number throughout my life, my practical experiences have brought me time and again to the number 8. My first baseball hero was Carl Yastrzemski, and he wore that number 8 around on his back for the duration of his career with the Boston Red Sox, which included leading the American League in batting average, home runs and runs batted in (the three categories it takes to win baseball's Triple Crown) in 1967, when I was six years old.

My first year playing baseball, I was issued a jersey with the number 8 on it. It all happened quite coincidentally. As it happened, the eight-year old team's uniforms at the Mountair Little League, just west of Denver, had two jerseys with the number 8 on it. Danny Frost and I were handed the jerseys. Somehow, I was offered the opportunity to change to another jersey (Danny was the coach's son), and I just told them I would have my Mom iron on a "0" to the right of the 8 for the rest of that year. For my first year of organized baseball, I was number 80. Eventually, Danny's mom ironed a "1" to the left of his 8, making him 18. So we both got a piece of number 8. I don't remember why Danny liked number 8, but it must have been a good compromise, because Danny and I were friends throughout the year, and for a couple years after that.

But as I roll into my 50s playing slow pitch softball, the number 8 on my jersey remains—without the ironed-on additions.

I also kind of like the idea that if the number 8 were to fall over, it would look like the symbol for infinity. We'd all like to play forever, if only our bodies would comply. I've also had a soft spot for 7 and 3 over the course of my life, and I have won a few random guesses with these numbers (dumb luck), so I like to stick with them. I have never won a game of number-guessing by choosing 4 or 6. Of course, I don't think I've ever offered a guess with either of those numbers, so it would logically be impossible to win. While it is also impossible to go back and tally each of the times I picked my number, in reality, my "lucky" numbers probably only produced their predictable share of victories, in spite of my propensity to pick them all the time.

You likely have a similar story with different numbers.

Never underestimate the human ability to revise history to fit our superstitions. Anyone can choose selected events in history to fit their belief systems. This is a universal truth in the mystical world of superstition, and probably the entirety of luck itself.

Ask anyone at the keno parlor whether they have a set of lucky numbers. Pull up a chair and prepare to hear a story. Your children's birth dates, perhaps? Maybe your regular numbers are a set of digits representing an important date in your life? We all have them, whether we adhere to them ardently or not. As you prepare to buy a Powerball ticket when the jackpot rises beyond $100 million, do you have a predetermined set of numbers you will use? Or will you simply let the computer choose those numbers for you? Either way, your scientific odds of winning are just as astronomical. On the other hand, have you ever just allowed the computer to pick your numbers only to see most of your "regular" numbers come in? How badly can that make you feel? Better to just stick with your regular numbers rather than to have them come in while you were courting luck with some rogue set.

In December of 2013, a Gretna, Nebraska couple won the Powerball jackpot after diligently buying tickets twice a week for many years using the same set of numbers, based on birth dates in the family. One day, David Harrig inadvertently filled out his ticket with all of his family's birthdates and his own lucky number—three. Except when he went to blacken the three, his marking pencil went inexplicably to the number one instead. That "mistake" made the Harrigs winners of the $61 million dollars (before taxes) jackpot.

"Some people call it a mistake, some people call it a miracle. My friends have called it my IQ," David Harrig said at a news conference, explaining why he darkened the number one box.

Is this numerology, or the hand of God intervening? Why did the tip of his pencil go to the "wrong" box? Why did he allow it? He could have thrown his form away and started over. If we studied the situation long enough, we could come up with something that made numerologic sense, but I'll bet it wouldn't be reliable enough to choose next week's winning numbers. Sometimes we just don't know which forces are in play. It just seems like an honest mistake at the moment, so we hardly give it a second thought—until lightning strikes (the odds of winning the Powerball are often compared to your odds of being struck by lightning—with the lightning strike being the slightly better bet).

The deference, good and bad, to numbers has also bled into our culture.

For some reason, while many in our culture claim Friday the 13th to be an unlucky day, I have always survived the 13th just fine, only to have things go sour on Saturday the 14th.

It appears as if the "Friday the 13th" superstition may be merely an amalgamation of two older superstitions. In numerology, the number 12 is considered the number of divine organizational arrangement. Jesus had twelve apostles. Muhammed had twelve successors. There are twelve signs of the zodiac. Thirteen, however, is considered irregular, thus transgressing this completeness.

Urban planners have continued the myth. Many cities do not have a 13th Street or 13th Avenue. Many buildings do not have a 13th floor. The legend grows as numerologists note that Charles Manson, Jeffrey Dahmer, Theodore Bundy and Osama bin Laden all have thirteen letters in their names. To me, the mass murderer angle sounds more like reconstructing history to fit your beliefs.

Friday has always carried a cloud over it as the day of the week Jesus was crucified, shortly after the Last Supper, where thirteen people were at the table. Certain legends (and I heard this repeated by several farmers) report that Friday is an unlucky day to start a journey or a new project. We can't be sure how much of this legend is rooted in getting the best camping spots at the lake by showing up on Thursday night.

So when you put the clouds of Friday on top of the curse of the number 13, you really have the convergence of multiple superstitions for people to fear—and to propagate the legend.

People trying to correlate numbers with good and bad luck are found worldwide where the obtaining of "lucky" *telephone numbers,* automobile *license plate* numbers, and *household addresses* are actively sought, sometimes at great *monetary* expense. Millions of people throughout America pay extra to get a specific license plate number or message for their car. Admittedly, some of that is just pure vanity, but there is often a root of a lucky number or lucky phrase on the plate somewhere.

Why do "bad things always happen in threes?" The death of public figures, or a group of friends or family members, seem to cluster into threes. I have often sensed an air of uneasiness as people gather at the second funeral of the week among a common group. "Who will be number three?" is the unspoken question.

Still, three serves as a magical number in the human psyche when it comes to laughter. Any good joke-teller knows the value of the three-stage joke. "A brunette, a redhead, and a blonde walk into a bar . . ." Two people will play it straight, and the third person in the story delivers the punch line. It's Comedy 101. It keeps the set-up time for any joke short enough that our attention spans can be fully engaged. Others would say, the three-stage joke allows you to make your point and move on. Depends on how hard they laughed.

Like astrologists, numerologists fashion their craft to be more of an art than a science. This is an admission to the fact that we can't really physically identify the source of this power. On the other hand, everyone is obliged to support their particular pursuit of the fates.

The people working the art of "seeing the future" want you to believe the forces at play are understandable, rational and predictable. The more dispassionate and mechanical the theory seems to be, the more science you can squeeze into the back door of the discussion. Still, there is much disagreement among the various psychics about just where numerology rates in its effectiveness. Of course, everyone needs to defend their window into the cosmos. It also helps if you cast a little suspicion on any competing fortune-teller's method.

Obviously, there are no numbers that are going to come up substantially more often than others in a random shuffle, but if you know the favored number of the person who gets to select the "random" number to be guessed between one and ten, you might have an inside track on a system to beat the odds. Otherwise, we just choose a number with which we are comfortable . . . and sometimes it comes in.

On those days, we feel lucky. If you are playing the Powerball when your numbers come in, it can change your life (although nearly everyone insists it won't).

REFLECTION QUESTIONS

What "lucky numbers" have you used throughout your life? How did you choose those numbers?

Have you changed numbers over time?

CHAPTER 7

LUCK AS A LIFE RESPONSE

"I know what you're thinking, punk. You're thinking did he fire six shots or only five? And to tell you the truth, I forgot myself in all this excitement. But being this is a .44 Magnum, the most powerful handgun in the world, and will blow your head clean off, you've got to ask yourself a question. Do I feel lucky? Well, do you, punk?"

—Clint Eastwood as Dirty Harry

"I'm a greater believer in luck, and I find the harder I work the more I have of it."

— Thomas Jefferson

While we have talked about luck as the result of heavenly or cosmic forces converging upon us, for better or worse, there is another viewpoint that defines luck as merely the result of the energy we bring into any situation.

That is, if we approach any situation feeling good about the possibilities and looking for a small pebble of goodness to start an avalanche, then good fortune suddenly descends upon an individual, seemingly out of nowhere. The Life Response proponents postulate that luck is not a haphazard and random phenomenon, but follows identifiable patterns and principles of life.

People believing luck is a life response fundamentally believe that the luck which comes our way is due to a shift in one's consciousness to a higher plane in a moment or circumstance. They say the outcome is rooted in the principle of "inner-outer correspondence," which states that life outside our self is a reflection of our inner condition. Therefore, Roy Posner says, if we *raise our consciousness in some manner, life quickly responds in kind, as we move in alignment with corresponding positive conditions.*"

Posner provides many interesting observations about how we might "make our own luck" in life. He has done over 350 essays on human evolution and transformation. He attempts to merge the scientific, the cosmic, and the spiritual into a complex matrix, which makes strides toward the crux of the matter of luck.

ON THE NATURE OF LUCK,
BY ROY POSNER

http://www.gurusoftware.com/GuruNet/KnowledgeBase/Personal/
SpiritualQualities/Luck.htm

Luck is really just another name for "life response," i.e. good fortune suddenly or rapidly descending on an individual from seemingly out of nowhere. Thus, luck, life response, good fortune, attraction are different names for the same phenomenon. Moreover, Luck is not a haphazard and random phenomenon, but follows identifiable patterns and principles of life.

Then what is the cause of Luck? It is due to a shift in one's consciousness to a higher plane in a moment or circumstance. And that outcome is rooted in the principle of "inner-outer correspondence." It states that life outside ourselves is a reflection of our inner condition. Therefore, if we raise our consciousness in some manner, life quickly responds in kind, as we move in alignment with corresponding positive conditions.

Luck therefore is not what happens serendipitously, coincidentally, randomly, or per chance; but is rather a product of our inner condition in a given moment in time, or over a longer period. (By the way, this also works in the reverse. When there is a lower or lessening of one's consciousness, we attract ill-fortune—i.e. we become unlucky.)

Then what about people who are said to have special power to evoke Luck? Well, it is true that we are each born into this world with different levels of consciousness (knowledge, skill capacity, character, energy, etc.). Some individuals are even said to have an old or ripe soul, while others are known to have a child soul. Natively, the former attracts Luck, while the latter have the potential to do so.

Also, those who develop a steady will to develop themselves, inwardly and outwardly, tend to attract good fortune; i.e. evoke Luck into their lives. This is the path or progress open to each and every one of us.

Then there are certain individuals who have a great destiny; who are linked to universal vibrations, and their actions—psychological and physical—evoke powerful response from life. Winston Churchill and Bill Gates come to mind.

One other interesting aspect of Luck is that it occasionally happens in waves as one goes through what one considers a "lucky period." What would account for this dynamic? It must be because our consciousness has risen to a tipping point relative to circumstance, which concentrates and releases a great amount of energy, which attracts a plethora of good fortune from a number of quarters. Tracking, measuring, and understanding such bursts of luck/good

fortune would make a fascinating study, and would help
us evoke waves of Luck of our own. "

Richard Wiseman, a psychologist at the University of Hertfordshire, has conducted significant research to determine how people frame their brushes with luck, and why some people just seem to experience more good luck than bad. "My research revealed that lucky people generate good fortune via four basic principles. They are skilled at creating and noticing chance opportunities, making lucky decisions by listening to their intuition, creating self-fulfilling prophesies via positive expectations, and adopting a resilient attitude that transforms bad luck into good," he says.

Wiseman also shares three observations about the differences between the lucky and unlucky among us.

* *"Unlucky people often fail to follow their intuition when making a choice, whereas lucky people tend to respect hunches. Lucky people are interested in how they both think and feel about the various options, rather than simply looking at the rational side of the situation. I think this helps them because gut feelings act as an alarm bell - a reason to consider a decision carefully.*

* *Unlucky people tend to be creatures of routine. They tend to take the same route to and from work and talk to the same types of people at parties. In contrast, many lucky people try to introduce variety into their lives. For example, one person described how he thought of a color before arriving at a party and then introduced himself to people wearing that*

color. This kind of behaviour boosts the likelihood of chance opportunities by introducing variety.

- *Lucky people tend to see the positive side of their ill fortune. They imagine how things could have been worse. In one interview, a lucky volunteer arrived with his leg in a plaster cast and described how he had fallen down a flight of stairs. I asked him whether he still felt lucky and he cheerfully explained that he felt luckier than before. As he pointed out, he could have broken his neck."*

Richard Wiseman, The Telegraph, 09 Jan 2003
http://www.telegraph.co.uk/technology/3304496/Be-lucky-its-an-easy-skill-to-learn.html

Luck, according to this line of thought, is not what happens seren-dipitously, coincidentally, randomly, or per chance; but is rather a product of our inner condition in a given moment in time, or over a longer period. Similarly, when there is a lower or lessening of one's consciousness, we attract ill-fortune—i.e. we become unlucky.

We all know people who mope around in life, just waiting for the next worldly injustice to fall in their lap. "Why does this always happen to me?" is the common sigh of resignation.

We also know people who go through life waiting for the next thing to humor them, or the next thing that will bring some joy into their lives. Any misfortune that does arrive simply presents itself as a new opportunity to make lemonade out of the lemons delivered.

In essence, it appears to these folks as if an individual's good or bad luck is merely the embodiment of whether optimism or anxiety rules your brain. Does a particular turn of events send you spiraling into depression, or does it energize you to find the good in the situation?

Luck may only provide us with an easy way to describe the situation, because we can really point to no more meaningful cause for the outcome. Indeed, our luck in many situations may be shaped by our attitude, and the way we tell the story.

It is said whatever you focus on in life expands. There is much to be said for that little axiom. Indeed, we all have things we *have* to pay attention to in life: perhaps a growing tumor, the rapidly approaching brick wall, or the children whose mouths will need to be fed for many years until they are able to earn their own money to purchase and prepare their own food. But how we approach the challenges with which we are faced can go a long way toward shaping (or at least framing) the possible outcomes.

This position concedes great power to the individual to overcome the forces of astrology, the will of God, or the tenets of superstition. It does, moreover, create a scenario in which your outlook on life is more pivotal to the success of your endeavor than any external forces.

Nowhere does this philosophy present itself to me more clearly than through my friend, Dave Temple.

Dave was a strapping young son of a State Patrolman who grew up in northeast Nebraska. He aspired to be a veterinarian, and was attending school at Kansas State University when fate came to call.

It happened on a June evening when he was driving home after a long day. The drive was long and the hour was late.

The long, dark road peeled by his vehicle in a soothing manner. The steady hum of his tires on the pavement proved a little too soothing, however, as he drifted off to sleep behind the wheel. His vehicle crossed the center line of the road, and by the time he regained consciousness, he yanked the wheel just in time to miss a tree, but he didn't miss the culvert in a roadside ditch.

No air bags and an unused seat belt contributed to the catastrophic nature of his injuries.

The collision caused him to injure his spinal cord between the fifth and sixth vertebrae. More importantly, it rendered him a quadriplegic, with very little feeling or control of his body below his shoulders. He is now unable to fully control his bowels or bladder without help from an array of medical interventions. He has trouble regulating his body temperature, the way most of us humans can, because his body doesn't perspire.

He has developed new routines that make the most out of his difficult situation, but he spends much more time than most changing his clothes when somehow, someway, he springs a leak in his condom-style catheter/leg bag appliance that catches his urine (as luck would sometimes have it, just as he is going out the door to an appointment).

His accident certainly changed the direction and outlook of his life for the frustrating. Many of us would understand if a traumatic episode such as this might cause him to just quit trying to live an independent life. After an extended round of soul-searching, he found a way to forge an amended outlook on life, and for that at least, he can feel fortunate.

After much rehabilitation, Dave has found a way to live as independently as possible and carry on with the life that remains. Every time he gets into bed, gets in the shower, sits on the toilet, or gets into his van, he must hoist himself from his wheelchair to his next destination. If he misses or slips on any one of those transfers, he can fall to the floor—and remain there until someone comes by to lift him back into his chair. His van is equipped with a lift and a power seat base, which allow him to enter from the side, transfer to the driver's seat, and spin around into position to drive.

He is certainly the picture of determination, as he pulls up in his GMC Safari van. At first, as his side door slides open and the lift folds out, he is a curiosity. He bristles at the first impression. Most times he would like to just blend into the crowd, but he doesn't let that deter him.

Many people have called him lucky over the years, and when he pauses to survey what he has in life, he too says, "I am a lucky boy." But there are many days when he feels anything but lucky. Frustration is never too far afield for a guy who is paralyzed from the shoulders down, and it is often too easy to choose the easy route through your day when you've expended most of your energy just to run a bowel program and get dressed.

While Dave doesn't regularly qualify for in-home attendant care (he pays out of his own pocket for help to come in twice a week), he feels infinitely fortunate to have the support of friends and family.

It is said that, in order to maintain independence, disabled persons each need three to seven people in their lives who can be called on to provide various forms of assistance. Perhaps that axiom is also true for those of us without such physical limitations, but it is particularly true for the disabled.

Many of the tasks we able-bodied take for granted might, on any given day, generate the need for a less-able person to need a helping hand. Any chore from taking out the trash and vacuuming, to mowing the lawn, to assisting with transfers, to picking up prescriptions could arise on a given day as a pressing need for someone confined to a wheelchair.

It is a commitment for his legion of helpers to check in regularly, and to be on-call should he end up on the floor as the result of a bad transfer. It is humbling to be so dependent, but he is very lucky to have a group of people who are alternately willing and able to answer his calls.

In new social settings, Dave is often seen as a curiosity. Guys mostly look over the top of him. Some girls assume the Florence Nightingale pose and treat him as someone to be pitied and coddled. Kids are often scared to approach him at first, and then want to play with the wheelchair. It *is* a pretty cool instrument.

Once people get to know him a little bit, they often describe him as an inspiration. After all, he has overcome more than most of us can imagine, and he is still trying to participate in society.

"I hate being considered inspiring," he often says. "I'm just doing what I have to do to survive from day to day. Just like you or anyone else would."

I believe that many of us may not be as determined as Dave has been, to remain active and independent in the face of his challenges. Many of us would just want to roll out in front of a speeding bus and be done with it. But that would create an unlucky day for the bus driver, and other innocent passers-by.

That he hasn't chosen to quit is regularly inspiring to me and others, but that is not why he does what he does.

While many people in human history have conjured up the will and determination to create great things in the world, Dave must draw on the same dogged determination to get out of bed, make and eat breakfast, gather his clothes, transfer back into bed, make sure his catheter and leg bag are still functioning adequately, get dressed while lying in bed, button and zip his pants without the benefit of a working opposable thumb, transfer back out of bed, brush his teeth, get out the front door, lower his van lift, transfer onto his car seat, and drive his van across town using hand controls—all without compromising his catheter, which would cause his leg bag to drain out all over his jeans.

What happens once he arrives at his destination is usually a new adventure. Can he even get into the building? Will there be available parking on a level surface? There are dozens of opportunities for luck to rear its head in his life—for good or for bad—in a simple visit to the grocery store. Try maneuvering a shopping cart from the seat of a wheelchair sometime. Don't even think about getting to those cookies on the top shelf.

Accommodations have been greatly improved for the handicapped, but as a society we still have a fair distance to go for total accessibility. Just try getting a tightened lid off of a jar with one functional hand and a marginal grip. Modern food packaging often defies a disabled person from enjoying the treats inside. He has learned some new uses for scissors, and letter openers, and yard sticks. Ever imagine how a wheelchair-bound person can get between the car and the curb at a gas pump? It isn't always easy.

There is so much that those of us with a full complement of working limbs take for granted physically. And of course, there are the social implications of being disabled.

Dave did get married once, but it only lasted a few years. The work involved in living with a quadriplegic was more than his bride had bargained for, not to mention his tendency to be more of a "home body," because going out for any reason always brings with it a ton of work. If you have a general predisposition of getting out to socialize on a regular basis, living with a wheelchair-bound person is going to put a damper on that. Unless you just decide to go out by yourself, which provides you with the opportunity to meet others who don't have an aversion to an active lifestyle. His wife took that path, met another person without a physical disability, and the rest is a sad story that builds on his challenges in life.

But being married did inspire Dave to take a job as student ombudsman at the University of Nebraska, which led to him buying a house.

It also enabled him to secure a policy for disability insurance, which, despite his pre-existing condition, was issued happily.

When his health took a turn for the worse with a kidney and bladder infection several years later, he was granted the permanent disability designation which now helps him live month-to-month and make the mortgage payment on the small house in which he still lives. All in all, while his marriage ended badly, it did leave him with remnants, allowing him to continue living relatively independently. Really, Dave realized a pretty lucky result in the face of a devastating time in his personal life.

But now, as a single man again, the challenge of getting out to interact with people remains. Meeting women in the first place, as a quadriplegic, is difficult. Boys in wheelchairs are at a distinct disadvantage meeting girls in a bar. The act of bending over to talk to a wheelchair-bound man offers a little too much "exposure" for a lot of the girls who might have a passing interest in the soul in the chair. Also, so much of the courting ritual involves seeing the prospective mate as healthy, strong and virile. It's a hard set of criteria to live up to when you roll onto the scene in a wheelchair.

His ideal woman would be tall and strong, and be willing to provide a certain amount of attendant care for him on a regular basis. That is not a universally appealing dowry to bring into a relationship.

Whatever "luck" Dave has realized over the years since his injury (after the fact that he sustained his disability at a point in the evolution of medical science where someone could survive such a trauma) has been almost solely due to his own disposition.

"The fact that I am in this situation is my own damn fault," he often says. "Life is always easier when you have someone (or something) else to blame. But usually we have no one to blame but ourselves."

This is not to say Dave doesn't harbor character traits that inhibit him from further success day-to-day. His industrial-strength pro-crastination gene is always present, and it is sometimes fed by the difficulty he anticipates with even the most routine tasks.

Still, he dreams of the day when modern medicine can help him walk again. Whether or not that happens in his lifetime, he still dreams of racing at the salt flats of Bonneville and careening around the hairpin turns at the Pikes Peak Hill Climb. Given where he has come from, I would hesitate to bet against him realizing those dreams. But if he gets to the top of Pikes Peak, no matter the time he ultimately records, he will certainly have climbed further to ascend that hill than anyone else in the race.

REFLECTION QUESTIONS

How has a disability inhibited or inspired you (or someone close to you)?

How many people can you call on for support when in need?

How many people call on you to provide support when in need?

TAKING RESPONSIBILITY
FOR OUR OWN LUCK

"We are taught you must blame your father, your sisters, your brothers, the school, the teachers - but never blame yourself. It's never your fault. But it's always your fault, because if you wanted to change you're the one who has got to change."

— **Katharine Hepburn**

Assigning luck to your responses in life happens in many less traumatic situations. You've probably known people who just can't seem to get out of their own way. There are people who sabotage themselves with addictive behaviors or a flight reflex. Others just don't have a regulator on their voice box. They don't know when everything *doesn't* need to be said, and in the process, they incite others to contribute to their string of bad luck.

I've done many silly things in life that have come back to bite me. At the top of my current list is my decision to quit a perfectly good, if somewhat unfulfilling, job after nearly twenty-three years of loyal service.

One ugly turn after another accompanied a change in leadership— and a change in the alliances within the office. No doubt, I should have been more vocal in my opinions as the situation developed and offered my advice more insistently. But given the criminal and ethical misdeeds that were committed by the people in the organization, I found it easier to just do my job day-to-day and hope that the whole sordid affair would blow over.

While I was keeping my head down, a new workplace order emerged, to whom I was an uncomfortable reminder of the past. I became a piece of the organization the leadership really would rather do without. Also, once I uncovered the entirety of the misdeeds, I figured I had three ways to move forward: Blow the whistle, become a co-conspirator to the cover-up, or quit and look for something else to do.

I chose the latter.

In retrospect, I should have stood firm on the principles of the matter. The worst that could have happened is that I would still be unemployed, but maybe with a little better severance package to soften my transition a bit. Instead, I gave the leaders a gift and resigned.

What my decision got me was a position on the long bench of middle-aged professionals who appear too old and too expensive to fill the professional-level jobs in the marketplace, too qualified for hourly work at the Home Depot, and too young and ill-prepared financially to retire.

I would like to selfishly claim this position exclusively for myself, but I have seen many of my friends and acquaintances go through the same personal meat-grinder. Over a couple of decades in the workplace, you can't help but develop and hone a certain skill set. Finding a place to transplant that skill set is often very difficult.

I now find myself competing with applicants who are my children's age. They don't know a fraction of what I've learned, but some percentage of what I've learned is obsolete. What's more, the idealistic glow in the eyes of a person about to get their first "real" job is inspiring to prospective employers. It takes a while to put all of that experience in the back seat and demonstrate that you, too, can still be molded in the company's image.

Just because we reach our fifties, and understand that molding ourselves into a particular company's image provides no guarantees of long-term happiness (depending on the company and its image), doesn't mean we can stop playing the game. I've always seen the process of interviewing for a job as a two-way street. Certainly, the employer is searching for an employee that will fit their mold. At the same time, the employee has an equally important task of finding out whether the company fits his or her vision for a place in which it is rewarding and fun to work. But too often, it comes down to a simple decision of whether you can stand to do the work.

Some people can never find a place where they are comfortable, which results in an almost never-ending string of job changes.

In the final analysis, my midlife employment crisis is something I brought upon myself. On the surface, it looks like some of the worst luck possible. Whether the cause of my unemployment was my over-active conscience—or a covert effort to "clean the slate" by my former employer—doesn't really matter for the rest of my life moving forward (except, perhaps, for the resulting karma). Looking back on our lives is mostly wasted energy, except as a means to avoid making similar mistakes in the future.

On the other hand, quitting my "career job" has provided me an opportunity to write a book, clear my conscience, lessen my stress, and dream of what else I might be able to do. Since I made that fateful decision, I have worked as an book author, a television reporter, a bartender at a microbrewery, sold everything from lawnmowers to printing services, and worked with a home remodeling business where I have learned many lifelong skills. Indeed, I now look back on my departure from my first chosen career as one of the luckiest decisions of my adult life. After working for 25 years with governors, senators, and school superintendents, I relish the opportunity to work with a diverse lineup of other interesting people that I would not have likely come into contact with otherwise.

To be sure, there were moments when I (and others) questioned the wisdom of my resignation, but I now believe it was a very fortuitous decision.

I witnessed early lessons in making my own luck all the way back in high school. The very meaning of making your own luck was embodied by an energetic classmate of mine named Mike Sloat. When he was a freshman, "Sloat" (as we all called him not-always-so-affectionately) had one fundamental problem, he had the mouth of a big man who wasn't afraid of anybody, but it was trapped inside the body of the boy who was about 5-foot-2 and 98 pounds. The poor kid got himself shut into more lockers, and constantly positioned him as the butt of the upperclassmen's derision. While I mostly found his bombastic stories rather annoying, most of the other freshmen were quick to identify Sloat as someone even *they* could look down on. Everyone needs that, at some point in life. As long as Sloat was around, the chances the rest of us would suffer the ire of the upperclassmen were greatly diminished. I always felt more comfortable because the more freshmen who popped off at inopportune times, the easier I found it to blend into the cinder block walls of the gymnasium.

I remember Sloat used to tell everyone that his doctor had informed his parents he was going to be 6-foot-4 when he was done growing. After that proclamation, the seniors promptly rolled him up in the wrestling mat and left the gym.

As an interesting side note, I saw Mike Sloat at our 20-year class reunion . . . and he is about 6-foot-4, and he is a pretty nice guy. At least he finally grew into his mouth.

By brazenly asserting a pompous approach in his encounters with the seniors, however, Sloat taught me that it helps to keep your head down and avoid attracting bad luck. It taught me to believe you can at least minimize your exposure to the worst of luck by choosing your words (and actions) very carefully.

Of course, I haven't always remembered that little lesson throughout my life, but there is usually no delay in the friendly reminders I receive through somebody's unexpected violent reaction to my words. Just because nobody is really listening to us some percentage of the time doesn't mean they cannot decide to tune into the monologue coming out of your mouth at any given time. More than anything, this human phenomenon has convinced me that listening is a much more important life skill than talking.

It is also worth learning that we should "let a sleeping bear lie," if we are not willing to manage the consequences of stirring up trouble. I think Sloat (and probably each one of us) could avoid a bunch of trouble, if we were aware of the potential perils we might be leading ourselves into. If I had known that quitting my job would mean more than a year of unemployment, it certainly would have had some influence on my decision. It is convenient to blame luck on our own lack of awareness. After all, everyone needs something (or someone) to blame.

Then again, if you know the flame is hot and you still burn your finger, you could rightfully be called more stupid than lucky. With all of the information before you, it is often your intelligence that is put to the test, instead of your luck.

At the same time, perhaps it is our experiences that cause us to be overly cautious when the next opportunity arises. While we are licking our wounds from the last encounter, along comes another opportunity to succeed or fail. With the predisposition that we are "having a bad day," we approach the next situation timidly, just waiting for something to go wrong. At the first hint of trouble, we shut down and sigh, "This just isn't my day."

Not with an attitude like that it isn't, young man.

How's Your Karma?

(Karma: as defined by Wikipedia Encyclopedia)
http:// http://en.wikipedia.org/wiki/Karma#Definition_and_meanings)

"Karma is the executed 'deed', 'work', 'action', or 'act', and it is also the 'object', the 'intent'. Halbfass[3] explains karma (Karman) by contrasting it with another Sanskrit word kriya. The word kriya is the activity along with the steps and effort in action, while karma is (1) the executed action as a consequence of that activity, as well as (2) the intention of the actor behind an executed action or a planned action (described by some scholars[16] as metaphysical residue left in the actor). A good action creates good karma, as does good intent. A bad action creates bad karma, as does bad intent.[3]

"Karma, also refers to a conceptual principle that originated in India, often descriptively called the principle of karma, sometimes as the karma theory or the law of karma.[17] In the context of theory, karma is complex and difficult to define.[18] Different schools of Indologists derive differ-

ent definitions for the karma concept from ancient Indian texts; their definition is some combination of (1) causality that may be ethical or non-ethical; (2) ethicization, that is, good or bad actions have consequences; and (3) rebirth.[18][19] Other Indologists include in the meaning of karma that which explains the present circumstances of an individual with reference to his or her actions in past. These actions may be those in a person's current life, or, in some schools of Indian traditions, possibly actions in their past lives; furthermore, the consequences may result in current life, or a person's future lives.[18][20]"

3   Halbfass, Wilhelm (2000), Karma und Wiedergeburt im indischen Denken, Diederichs, München, Germany

16   Karl Potter (1964), The Naturalistic Principle of Karma, Philosophy East and West, Vol. 14, No. 1 (Apr., 1964), pp. 39-49

17 and 18 Wendy D. O'Flaherty (1980), Karma and Rebirth in Classical Indian Traditions, University of California Press, ISBN 978-0520039230, pp xi-xxv (Introduction); 18 at pp.3-37.

19   Karl Potter (1980), in Karma and Rebirth in Classical Indian Traditions (O'Flaherty, Editor), University of California Press, ISBN 978-0520039230, pp 241-267

20   Jeffrey Brodd (2009), World Religions: A Voyage of Discovery, Saint Mary's Press, ISBN 978-0884899976, pp. 47

I'm really unsure how to categorize karma among our four origins of luck. In many ways, it should be the "poster child" for the idea that your actions create the luck you must live with, but from its origins, it has been promoted as a force of nature. And yet, it has been advanced into our culture by Buddha and other religions, as one of the natural laws of the mind—just as gravity is a law of matter. Other describe karma as a physical law of nature, created by God, in His (or Her) attempt to create a divine system of justice that is self-governing and infinitely fair. It automatically creates the appropriate future experience in response to the current action.

No matter its origins, any study of luck can ill-afford to ignore karma.

Karma is used by people in our society as a way of explaining the outcome of a situation resulting the way it did, even though it could have easily ended differently. Karma, on its surface, seems to be presented as a comprehensive spreadsheet for your actions. In reality, it is a term referring to the cycle of cause-and-effect. It commands that we be mindful of our actions, words, and thoughts.

According to the theory of karma, what happens to a person, happens because he or she caused it by previous actions. It is about all the things a person has done, is doing, and will do. It basically amounts to a cosmic accountability system.

Karma describes our actions as seeds, which we are planting for harvest at a later date. Our actions are separated into the actions of the body (such as killing, stealing, and sexual misconduct), actions of speech (lying, divisive or harsh speech, and idle gossip), and the actions of the mind (craving, aversion, and delusion).

This concept of karma somewhat diminishes the existence of random luck, but it instead insists that the spoils (which might include short- or long-term consequences) will, in the end, go in favor of the person with the purest motives and the strongest work ethic. And for those of you who have ulterior motives or always seem to look for the easy way out, all I can say is, "Karma is a bitch."

Many *Western cultures* have notions similar to karma, often embodied in the phrase, *"what goes around comes around."* Christian expressions similar to karma include a biblical passage, "For he who sows to his own flesh will from the flesh reap corruption. But he who sows to the Spirit will from the Spirit reap eternal life" (*Galatians 6:7*). There is also the sage wisdom, "He who *lives by the sword, will die by the sword."*
Perhaps karma can be characterized as the forefather of the phrase, "you make your own luck."

Most South Asian religions embrace karma, which postulates that your present life situation is the result of actions you have committed in current or past lives. Additionally, how you conduct yourself in this life will have a bearing on how you will be reincarnated in future lives.

The "past and future lives" portion of karma is a real stretch for most of us. It demands the faith of accepting a system of perpetual life across the cosmos. This perpetual life concept replaces the traditional notion of Heaven and Hell as destinations for our souls upon our death. The jury is still out as to whether going to Hell or reincarnating as a household spider or mouse would be worse. I have been somewhat negligent in allowing spiders and mice a dignified space in this world.

It is generally more than enough for us to manage the affairs directly before us on this planet, without trying to concern ourselves with parallel universes we might—or might soon—inhabit.

While I have confessed to having only a loose affiliation with organized religion, I do believe in God. Mostly, I also believe that by the time we get to Judgment Day, we will all arrive about even on the "karma meter." If you had tremendous good happen to you, it is likely the result of good that you have created. If you treat somebody poorly, there will also be an offsetting ill effect you will have to overcome, or at least endure. I have not conducted a scientific study of this phenomenon, but when you live to fifty years, you can begin to see the tally sheets balance out for people in various parts of the world.

Richard Nixon, Jim and Tammy Bakker, Pee Wee Herman, and Donald Trump are all examples of people in my lifetime who have soared to the top of their professional pursuits, only to find themselves destitute by a sudden change in the winds of favor. Some of these people recover from their public disgrace to rise again. Nixon accomplished this multiple times, only to implode more magnificently than the time before. Others are just unable to collect enough from the ashes of their careers to rebuild.

The existence of karma isn't always intuitive, and its presence doesn't mean you will never have any trouble. We've all seen good people get into bad situations and come out relatively unscathed. I've seen unsavory characters in difficult spots come out smelling like a rose. We've likely all had experiences where a seemingly good person died way too young (thus the quip, "Only the good die young"). With the limited number of facts before those of us serving as eyewitnesses, it seems unjust at certain moments that something comes out the way it does. But if the outcome is based on a lifelong accounting of deeds (and indeed, over a series of lifetimes), it is possible that the winner of a particular confrontation deserved to win after all—even if it didn't seem to be the case at that exact moment.

Believing in karma allows you the opportunity to not be so flabbergasted when you see an incredible turn of events in the news or otherwise. Within the horror of a hurricane or a terrorist attack, the act and the suffering seems so incomprehensibly unjust. But if there is a larger context from which this event is born, maybe it can begin to help justify where it comes from, and maybe where it will lead.

Unfortunately, none of us can get a true feeling for our life forces before we are about three years old, or after we are dead. So knowing exactly where we stand on the gigantic life-form recycling project is difficult, day-to-day. Still, the concept of "you reap what you sow" is valuable in guiding us through the many decisions we are faced with through life.

Karma encourages us to choose a path more suited to getting along with our fellow man. And it allows us to walk away from a negative encounter with some comfort that, sooner or later, today's bad seed will "get what they have coming to them."

Many people erroneously think of karma as a system of reward and punishment created by Buddha to allow the celestial being an opportunity to practice data-based decision making. But this is not true. Buddha did not create the system. By all accounts, he only discovered it. Rather, karma is framed as the description of a physical force in the mind, much as gravity or centrifugal forces bring order to the physical world.

Karma creates a system of cosmic justice that is self-governing and infinitely fair. It automatically creates the appropriate future experiences in response to the current action. If you plant the seeds of ill will, they will sprout as thorny trees. If you bring grace and happiness to those around you, it will result in a happier future for you. Whether these happy characterizations of karma are true or not, they provide a fine context from which to live your life.

Through a belief in karma, we can all carry our deeds on our own ledgers—our consciences. To the extent that we are honest with ourselves, it serves as the ultimate system of accountability. Our own abilities to reconstruct history serve as our only oasis, but the truth endures.

Looking at our previous assertion that luck is determined by how you react to a certain set of circumstances, karma provides us with an accounting system that is fluid and dynamic. You may find yourself, at any given time, somewhat ahead of the game, or somewhat behind. Nature's forces will eventually bring everyone to justice. Containing myself within the life I am currently living, I am left to wonder if I committed some impropriety from my early life that dictated that I was to come face-to-face with a chainsaw when I was seventeen years old. Not knowing what the karmic price list might look like, I cannot imagine what kind of transgression you would have to commit to earn an encounter with a chainsaw, but I will admit I was not perfect.

This has also caused me to wonder, did I disparage someone with a facial scar or other physical deformation in an earlier life? What kind of seed did my soul sow in a previous life, which earned me this badge on my cheek? I also considered whether, perhaps, the chain saw accident had the effect of paying forward my account, thus ensuring me a relative pool of good fortune throughout the balance of this life.

Not knowing the answer can be a torment, so I have just decided to assume the latter explanation.

Maybe our accounts can hold a balance, whereby one disfiguring accident can give you enough penance to last a lifetime. Therefore, all of the other misdeeds during my life will be covered because I not only endured the chainsaw incident, but I moved forward and even used it to motivate myself into a better place from time to time. Perhaps it was another in a series of divine tests, put before me to see if I had the gumption at the precipice of my adulthood to overcome the obstacles presented.

We can never know the absolute answer to questions such as these. We only really know what we believe—and hope that we are somewhere close to the truth.

It is easy to get impatient with the sometimes-delayed reaction of the karmic forces. It is particularly disheartening to watch someone who may not deserve it reel in the accolades. But be patient. There are many challenges to be faced in life, and today's winner will balance out in the end. Similarly, hard-luck losers will have their day—even if we have to wait until our reincarnation (in Heaven or on Earth) to realize it.

REFLECTION QUESTION

How have you seen karma work around you?

When it comes to karma, can we pay our debts in advance with the confidence that we will be reimbursed at some later point along our journeys?

CHAPTER 8

Dumb Luck

"Nobody gets justice. People only get good luck or bad luck."

— Orson Welles, Film Actor and Producer

"I'd rather be lucky than good."

— Lefty Gomez, Hall of Fame baseball pitcher

The final element is the least researched, but maybe the most interesting . . . dumb luck. Basically, dumb luck occurs when a set of circumstances arises, and things just seem to work out for the best. We do nothing to earn it, and we probably couldn't reproduce the result again if we were trying because our influence on the situation would, no doubt, change the outcome. Being the one-millionth customer, unless you have been spinning the turnstiles for three days, is just happenstance.

Occasionally, while in the drive-thru line at a fast food restaurant, I will pay for the food destined for the car behind me. Someone did this for me once, and I thought it was a pretty cool gesture. So, when it occurs to me, and I have to break a $20 bill anyway, I will do that. That simple act turns out to be dumb luck for the person behind me—and a good feeling for me. Maybe it improves my karma.

The employees who got detained from being at work on time at the World Trade Center on September 11, 2001, I contend, experienced an industrial-sized dose of dumb luck when the two jetliners crashed into the buildings and ultimately sent them tumbling to the ground with thousands of fastidiously prompt employees inside.

The WTC employees who were late that day, or maybe had a doctor's appointment to attend instead, will forever consider themselves lucky. Sometimes, a little dumb luck peeks into our lives to offset the corresponding circumstances.

A subset of dumb luck is affectionately called beginner's luck. Anyone who sits down to their first game of Yahtzee, dominoes, or Spades is subject to enjoy this warm experience. All you need is a serviceable knowledge of the rules and strategies of the game, and a friendly pair of dice, and you too can join the legions of newcomers who walk in and mop up the playing surface with veterans of Yahtzee wars.

Of course, it is worth noting that my research into beginner's luck has been somewhat skewed by my granddaughter, Teegan, who first deciphers the position in the game which makes you a winner, and then maneuvers all of her resources (legal and otherwise) toward that goal. Candy Land and Aggravation are games given to her shortcuts; we'll see how it works in card games when she gets old enough.

Every so often, we read about people who score a hole-in-one as novice golfers. Even for professional golfers, a hole-in-one demands a fair amount of luck. Yes, you have to hit the little dimpled ball far enough to get to a hole that is only 4.25 inches in diameter, and it usually has to be in the right general direction. However, the fickle nature of the bounce and roll are pivotal, if the ball is going to end its journey in the bottom of the cup.

I have played golf for more than thirty years. I have never scored a hole-in-one. I have holed out a couple of second shots from the fairway at a distance that would have been equal to a hole-in-one, but again, they were on my second shot. On the other hand, I never had to buy a round of drinks for everyone in the clubhouse; so maybe not experiencing a hole in one is a lucky thing—take the eagle and move on.

Just think, if you knocked in a hole-in-one on your first round, how would that skew your expectations of the game for the rest of your life? Golf is chock full of frustrations and disappointments, even without the irrational expectation that a hole-in-one is a regular occurrence.

Perhaps beginners' luck is made possible because you are simply not overthinking all of the details. Instead, we simply "let it rip" and let the consequences fall where they may.

But as for dumb luck, it most truly matches the Wikipedia definition, "*Luck or chance is an event which occurs beyond one's control, without regard to one's will, intention, or desired result."* It is truly out of our control. How else can you explain the way a tornado can move through a prairie town and destroy three houses on each side of a residence that stands relatively untouched?

If you are living in the house still standing, we would all have to agree you are lucky. The violence of a tornado is just too chaotic to imagine there is an architect behind it who methodically chooses who is damaged and who is not. As a survivor, you may understandably feel a little guilty at the plight of your neighbors, but it's hard to imagine that your life's good deeds saved you from the devastation bestowed upon the other sinners up and down the block. The people who survived the devastation at the World Trade Center on 9/11 were lauded as heroes, and yet it is a hollow feeling of accomplishment. They were all "lucky" in a way, but the catastrophic situation has created horrific visions that they all have to continue to live with.

Intermittently, we are also reminded of how lucky all of us Earth dwellers are when a giant asteroid takes aim on our home planet. We are blessed with an atmospheric shell, which dissolves a lot of space debris before it impacts the surface. But every now and again, our Earth crosses the path of a rock too big for our atmosphere to completely dissolve.

There are several locations around the Earth where the results of these impacts can be observed—many years after the fact. But several strikes within humanity's recorded history have demonstrated how the millions of chunks of rock floating in space can drastically alter all of the other elements we have stacked together, and describe as our lives. In Russia, a giant meteorite landed in Siberia in the early 20th century and leveled many square miles of forest. It's a fair bet that any manmade structure would also have been reduced to rubble. Luckily, the area was relatively uninhabited. It is said that a meteorite struck Earth on the Yucatan Peninsula in the Caribbean Sea many years ago. Some scientists believe a large strike on Mars many thousands of years ago, impacted its magnetic field and diminished much of its atmosphere. To date, we have no defense against such incursion, other than a thin layer of atmosphere, and our collective dumb luck.

Many of our soldiers returning from battle also have a difficult time when they are lucky enough to have survived their tour of duty. Physical and mental issues abound in a person who is involved in dozens of deadly hit-and-run battles over a series of months.

Why did the enemy's aim take out half of the platoon, but not hit them? The battlefield is littered with "what-ifs" and "if-onlys" that the soldiers in the field are left to pick up and bring home with them. When the stakes are life-and-death, and the bullets are flying, we understandably call on God, karma, astrology, superstition and anything else we can muster to help us survive. Whether or not luck is real or imagined, it becomes a close companion when people are shooting at you.

When the soldiers return home, it takes some time for many of them to settle into the work-a-day life of an accountant. But they are lucky for the opportunity, whether or not they are physiologically and psychologically up to it.

If you believe the world is generally a vast series of orderly forces converging on a set of circumstances, you could well see just about every turn of luck as simple dumb luck.

When you get in the way of flying objects, or power tools, they will occasionally hit you in the side of the head. After the fact, the impact can be seen as good or bad, perhaps, but certainly not unimaginable. Had you approached a given situation a little more aware of the world around you, the negative repercussions might have been avoided altogether.

But making those changes really doesn't make you "more lucky," just more cognizant of your surroundings.

REFLECTION QUESTION

How much of the luck we experience in life is just "dumb luck?"

Can you recall a case of beginner's luck in your life that you have been hard-pressed to recreate?

How much of dumb luck is simply our individual framing of an event?

CHAPTER 9

THE LUCKY FORCES INSIDE OF US

*"You know what luck is? Luck is believing you're lucky...
to hold front position in this rat-race you've got to believe
you're lucky."*

— Stanley Kowalski, A Streetcar Named Desire

TRUSTING YOUR INSTINCTS

"I have faith in my intuition, the language of my conscience, but I have no faith in speculation about Heaven and Hell."

— **Albert Einstein,**
Einstein and the Poet: In Search
of the Cosmic Man (1983)

We've all had an occasion in which, faced with several options, we just had a premonition that one choice was the right one. We can't make the conscious link as to why it is right, but "it sounds right" or "it jumps off the paper" to get our attention.

It isn't particularly a voice, but there is certainly some kind of force urging us to choose one answer over another, sometimes before we even get a chance to measure the relative merits of all the choices. Indeed, after doing an analysis of the situation, we may well choose an option that runs counter to our initial instinct.

And we usually find that we should have remained true to our first-blush impressions.

It's hard to say that there is a sub-channel running beneath our ability to readily perceive, providing us with the answers to many of our daily quandaries. It could just be a reflection of the way our brain processes information from our long-term memory. Then again, maybe it is God whispering in our ears.

Brain research has shown that we store information at three different levels. The flash memory allows you to interact with others instantaneously. It helps you remember what was just said so that you may respond to it as part of the conversation.

Short-term memory includes things such as grocery lists and directions. This block of memory allows us to act on information we receive within a short period of time to complete the task at hand. With repetition and context, items can eventually work their way into your long-term memory banks. Over time, the reason for remembering certain information grows insignificant, but bits of that information remain in your files, waiting for just the right instigator to bring the bit of information to the front of your brain.

How many people who grew up in the 1960s can, fifty years later, sing the opening theme song from the Gilligan's Island television program, which was played repetitively in syndication until the celluloid wore too thin to be useful (it's now been digitized and still pops up on the cable channels from time to time)?

How many other random tidbits of information have burrowed their way into our memory banks without our consent? The more random information you have in your head, the better it is, if you find yourself in a classic holiday game of Trivial Pursuit. How handy is it to know as a plain matter of fact which television program Art Fleming worked with Don Pardo to launch a game show dynasty?

More importantly, are we similarly embedded with bits of knowledge for which we have limited use—like driving a nail into wood, knowing the sequence of a wave pattern at the beach, or knowing generally that Ford and General Motors have historically created differences in their vehicles which give no functional advantage to anyone but their own certified mechanics? Why do many of us still know most of the addresses and phone numbers of the houses we lived in when we were growing up?

None of this information was particularly useful to prehistoric man, so it's difficult to blame genetics. Still, this information can occasionally be useful to us again. Somewhere down the road, we will run across a specific time when the information did have some recurring meaning to us—like with a multiple-choice question we couldn't have seen coming. When it does, one piece of information serves to ignite the long-term memory banks, and a little voice in our head says, "Pick B."

"Who was the original host and announcer of the television program 'Jeopardy!'?"

Is it possible that we are providing the programming for our own "sub-channel" with this holding tank of seemingly unconnected knowledge, which occasionally becomes extremely pertinent? If that is so, then is it our own insecurities causing us to doubt ourselves and overanalyze the situation with a "rational" eye? Things just aren't as rational as they should be sometimes.

As Obi-Wan Kenobi often implored young Luke Skywalker, as he developed through the Star Wars saga, "Trust your instincts, Luke." Perhaps that is because many of our instincts are based on personal experience and knowledge. Those experiences reveal facts we *know* are true, even if we might not have dealt with these truths for a very long time.

But to the people in a situation (and perhaps a land) far, far, away, others may well see your choice of answer, or reaction, to be incredibly lucky. "How did you pull that answer out of your hat?"

Truth is, you had been carrying that information under your hat for a very long time. It was just the convergence of time and opportunity, which came together to give you the appearance of a mystic.

In his book, "Blink," Malcolm Gladwell takes the power of trusting your first instincts to a higher level. He describes our brain's analysis during brief glances at a situation as "thin-slicing."

"Thin-slicing" describes the process by which our unconscious minds make choices about our actions and reactions based on a very thin set of experiences and information. Some people do this very well, and others are reckless in their application.

There may well be more than luck in the analysis that goes into our snap decisions. But often the criteria we are using to make our decision is guarded by a "locked door," as Gladwell says. It isn't always clear what the basis may be for our decisions. That our snap decisions are better than 50-50 indicates there is something more substantial there. But what it is still eludes us.

Gladwell notes, "We need to respect the fact that it is possible to know without knowing why we know and accept that—sometimes—we're better off that way" *(Blink, p. 52).*

People who are in a scholarly frame of mind have shown themselves to be more likely to answer a series of test questions correctly than a group of students who have just come from a discussion about the football game last night. If your mind is primed to the task currently before you, you are better able to make snap judgments about the current situation. A lot of this ability is just being in the right place at the right time, mentally.

Therefore, the circumstances surrounding your current situation can be more deftly handled if you are already thinking about the situation. Your brain already has begun to identify the bits of long-term memory that may be applicable, and allows you to come up with the right answer more often, even though it isn't resting on the tip of your tongue.

That may also be why—after some reflection—we are able to think up much better responses to a given question long after we have left the testing center. Our minds are toiling in the specific location of inquiry, allowing us to access those deeply filed thoughts that help us frame the correct response.

Listening to your instinctive knowledge can be very powerful, and may show you a way to success that, to others, may make you seem very lucky.

The Voice

"There's a voice that tells alcoholics we can drink. It's the same voice you hear if you go up to the top of the very tall building and look over the side. There's a little voice that goes, "Jump . . . You can fly!" Even though your asshole says, 'No you can't'!"

— Robin Williams

Relating to God's role in our lives, how do we process the reports that many people provide about hearing a "voice" advising them to move forward with one action or the other? Does the "voice" help us to be lucky in making the correct choice? Or do we convince ourselves that our decisions are correct because the "voice" told us to act in a certain way?

Is God chiming in at certain critical points in your life in order to fulfill his plan? Or is it the work of mystical spirits, perhaps originating from dearly departed relatives or maybe a previous occupant of the house? Or is it just an elaborate trick our brains are playing upon us to make us believe we have other-worldly guidance?

The voices in my head are mostly working in my internal jukebox. Nearly every morning, there is a song in my head that keeps rattling around throughout the day. I often join along in the shower as I find myself singing or whistling along with the seemingly random rotation of music accompanying me through my daily activities. That doesn't mean that, someday, my internal voice won't cut into the musical program in my head: "We interrupt this program for an important message about your life . . ."

But the voices apparently have (or create) other motivations inside the heads of others.

Notorious among the people who "hear voices" inside their head, are the criminals in our past, who report that they are merely following the direction of these "voices" when they commit any number of heinous crimes. These are ominously evil, and provide most of us with a simple explanation for the unthinkable crimes these people have committed. "They're just insane," is the clean and crisp answer that allows us to move on with our own personal version of reality. But are they simply obeying the voice?

But what about people who "hear a voice" very distinctly, but cannot identify its source. What about the people whose "voices" are instructing them to do something not-so-heinous. What if the "voice" is just providing us with non-specific guidance? The recorded origin of this phenomenon is at least chronicled as far back as Moses, who received a stone-aged accounting for all of the things "the Voice" imparted to him on that mountaintop so many years ago.

In any group of people, you can find several friends who have reported incidents of this sort. One of my friends noted that a voice once told him to go over and introduce himself to that girl on the other side of the room. Upon looking around, there was nobody close enough to him to be the source of that encouragement. A little haunted by the words he had just heard, he followed through and introduced himself to the young lady, who would eventually become his wife (the voice did not, by the way, tell him to marry her—but that's another story).

One of my former college roommates suffered a near-fatal episode after he turned fifty when an artery in his stomach ruptured. He was perilously close to death before the doctors were able to stabilize him and treat his condition. But while he was teetering between life and death, he reports hearing a voice that told him, "You are not done yet. You have more to do."

Back in his hospital bed, the memory of the voice burned deeply into his brain. Was that God? What better explanation can any of us have for such an experience? Perhaps the voice is generated from your inner being, urging you toward something to which your surface consciousness is not yet aware. Are we generating this experience from within, or is it indeed the voice of God?

While the source of this voice can be forever debated, our actions in response to these voices very often change our motivations and our outlook. It certainly provides us with an opportunity to treat our future with a determination that is stronger than anything we might have previously possessed. If we can use these events for the positive, we are likely to improve our lot in life. If the voices we hear urge us to "kill, kill, kill," we merely become a footnote in the journals of notorious mass murderers. In the former case, we can comfortably call it Divine intervention. In the latter, we feel better describing it as the work of the devil . . . or merely a case of mental illness.

For those of us who merely talk to ourselves about our daily challenges, perhaps we don't shut up long enough to delineate messages coming from external sources. These voices may well exist, but they do not penetrate the chatter of our daily lives. Perhaps they are the embodiment of the inner sanctums of our brains. Regardless of the source, they obviously drive people to make decisions about their lives that can later be described as either lucky or unlucky. This is quite possibly another simple explanation for something much more complex, but while the religious among us have an equally simple explanation, modern science has yet to put its finger on the exact origin of the voices.

Maybe it's just your inner luck trying to get out. If that is the case, maybe we should spend more time listening to the voices. Whether it is from God, some extraterrestrial forces, or a being from the after-life, or our inner voice, there may be something very important that somebody is trying to communicate to us. How we respond to those voices has often proven to be the difference between good and bad luck.

REFLECTION QUESTIONS

Have you (or someone you know) experienced the phenomenon of hearing a voice?

Did it create a change in your (their) behavior?

What do you believe is the source of "the voice?"

Luck's Dark Side

"I have never believed much in luck, and my sense of humor has tended to walk on the dark side."

— Hunter S. Thompson

"When you have a dark side, nothing is ever as good as it seems."

— Pink

Luck, of course, has a dark side as well. I have long thought there was some bad luck involved in placing me in the wrong place at the wrong time on that mountainside.

Why are some people just unlucky? Why does it resonate with us when blues master Albert King used to belt out, "If it wasn't for bad luck, I wouldn't have no luck at all?" Even among those of us who might classify ourselves as moderately lucky, we are all susceptible to "red light days." These are days when things just seem to fall the wrong way. We hit all the red lights on the way to work, and then the computer system goes down, and then you get a flat tire on the way home. The chain of events has spurred a number of sayings in our culture:

"When it rains it pours."

"Bad things always come in threes."

"It must be Murphy's Law."

Murphy's Law has unjustly come to serve as the godfather of bad luck in the popular culture. This Eeyore-like law states "anything that can go wrong will go wrong." Interestingly, the origin of Murphy's Law doesn't go back to the Emerald Isle. Instead, it apparently was created and took off during the test of the barriers of speed at Edwards Air Force Base in the 1950s.

From day one of the airplane testing in the California desert, there had been an unacknowledged but standard experimental protocol. The test team constantly challenged each other to think up "what ifs" and to recognize the potential causes of disaster. If you could predict all the possible things that could go wrong, the thinking went, you could also find a way to prevent catastrophe. And save a test pilot's life . . . or neck.

If anything can go wrong, it will. It was a concept that seized the cumulative imagination of the media covering these experiments, and it just took wing from there.

I have always associated Murphy's Law with the legion of unlucky people in the world. But its origin suggests there is more to it than that. If the fate of a prospective project is inevitably ominous, the task requires focused attention on the critical preparations and decisions that must be made to avoid disaster. So while Murphy's Law seems on its surface to be a little fatalistic, and has been twisted to appear more than a little self-defeating, it can also provide an outlook on life that makes it easier to accept the worst possible result (indeed, it calls on us to anticipate it) and move on.

In the case of the Air Force test pilots, the Law gave them the motivation to double-check, and play Devil's advocate, to all of the theories being tested as increasingly heavy G-forces were being exerted on their bodies. With that much at stake, there is no time to take anything for granted. If you think it could go wrong, the team should stop and talk about it to assess the situation. So in practice, Murphy's Law was originally used in an attempt to improve the luck of the test pilots. As it matured, it took on more of a negative outlook for those of us too lazy to double-check anything.

Once again, this element of the luck horizon can be used productively to reflect and reassess our situation and what we are trying to accomplish. If everything that can go wrong does, then perhaps we need to step back and analyze our strategy on the issue. What can we do to eliminate the things that can go wrong? Unfortunately, many of us use Murphy's Law to exercise the Eeyore in all of us. At times, it can even nix a prospective plan before it gets off the ground, as skepticism teams up with Murphy to create a barrier we find difficult to get around. Of course, it may have been a bad idea in the first place!

No matter which side of luck's pendulum we are struck by on a given day, the story of our lives will be written by the manner in which we respond to our unique situation.

A dear, older friend of mine, we called him Uncle Joseph (although he was not related to me, or any of my friends), left me with a wonderful axiom before he died, which has served me throughout my life. "You may know a lot of things, young man, but the most important thing you gotsta know is how to tuck and roll." It is true that, no matter how well you think your life is going, something somewhere is going to trip you up. When (not if) you fall, the most important element at play—in that instant—is whether you fall flat on your face, or if you roll your shoulder and use your momentum to get right back up on your feet and continue on your path.

While the "tuck and roll" advice tends to discount the role of luck in any mishap, I consider myself very lucky that Uncle Joseph was there to dispense this advice, and that I was smart enough to take it to heart. I have kept it close to my consciousness, and I have shared it with my children and others who often seem unable to extract themselves from a particular set of unfortunate circumstances.

In the end, Murphy's Law can create (or be the result of) a negative attitude, even though that was never the intention of the axiom's inventors. Move forward, but anticipate that anything can happen . . . and as I learned early in life, be ready to tuck-and-roll.

The "snowball effect" of bad luck is embodied in our education system. Students who fall behind their classmates in the curriculum often use the frustration of lagging behind to just stop trying. The frustration builds into a disdain for school, personal animosity toward the teacher and other students, and eventually a retreat into other alternative forms of entertainment (sometimes taking the form of drugs and alcohol).

In our fervor to create a uniform schedule by which all students ought to understand a certain percentage of a common curriculum at about the same point in their educational careers, we have created a system that cannot wait for laggards to catch up. The binder says we must move on. That is not insurmountable if the student is only mildly behind. But when they are significantly behind, it is easy for them to welcome hopelessness into their lives.

Bad luck is the right-hand man of hopelessness.

It is also possible that building a bad-luck portfolio for ourselves is simply a matter of reconstructing history. There have inevitably been positive turns of fate in everyone's life. But intent on building the hard-luck legacy, we ignore all of that and focus on the hurdles that impede us. Yes, the bad breaks do arrive. It is hard to deny that most of us are presented with imposing challenges in our worlds. But if our reaction is to sigh deeply and throw up our hands in resignation, the barriers can become insurmountable.

REFLECTION QUESTIONS

What are the barriers to luck you've built in your own life?

In what ways are you perpetually unlucky?

Working "In the Zone"

"But, he thought, I keep them with precision. Only I have no luck anymore. But who knows? Maybe today. Every day is a new day. It is better to be lucky. But I would rather be exact. Then when luck comes you are ready."

— **Ernest Hemingway**,
The Old Man and the Sea

Have you ever had a day when everything just came easy to you? When the lights all turned green just prior to your arrival at the intersection, and the parking space closest to the building is vacant and awaiting your arrival? What about those days when the people who you historically have a difficult time abiding just seem to see things your way?

When the good things come in rapid succession, we characterize that as being "in the zone."

Being "in the zone" is the best of times in sports. Your movements flow; you have a sense of where the other players are going; and your reflexes gear up a notch. Everything just seems to come easier. Athletes have reported seeing the ball much more clearly. The basket or goal seems to get a little bigger.

Even as I write this book, I notice that there are days when the words just flow. I have to be careful not to mix my thoughts as several ideas bubble to the surface in close proximity to each other. On other days, often in the same week, I cannot squeeze two paragraphs out of my fingers.

When someone finds their zone, it's obvious. They are eager to offer up their views. You can see the look in their eyes— they're the ones you want representing your team when the game is on the line. It's not because they're the fastest or the strongest. It's because they have found that extra something you can count on when the contest is close. The feeling of being in "the zone" may also come to a different person on your team in consecutive days. But can they get themselves in position to benefit your team?

When your concentration level peaks during an important point in your life, extraordinarily great things can be accomplished. But tomorrow, in the same situation, the results may not be the same.

The terms used to describe the "zone" phenomena vary. The sports psychology folks talk about visualization and relaxation response; the clinical hypnosis people sketch out trance levels; and medical doctors offer explanations of stress management.

Many of those practices can be combined into a concept called a Concentration Funnel. This funnel image describes a system of moving up and down your focus levels, moving from loose attention at the top to tight concentration at the bottom.

Working against us all are distractions to the things we must concentrate on. When those distractions begin to pile up against us on a given day, this phenomenon turns into what has been described as a "yellow-" or "red-light day." That's when the rain gets on the morning paper, your toast falls jelly-side-down on the kitchen floor and your shoe string breaks when you attempt to tie it.

Some days, you just hit all the yellow lights on the way to work, giving you a long string of decisions to make about how the rest of your day will seem.

People who are "in the zone" just seem more likely to avoid distractions and find the parking meter with time still on it, or get the benefit of the doubt when the result could fall either way.

Take the case of a professional baseball player. Every one of them has put in the hard work to get to where they are. From the Little

Leagues, through high school and college, the competition is always fierce, the travel gets extensive, and the self-discipline to improve skills gets more difficult as school, women and kids inflict their demands on an individual.

Along the way, every one of those players has hot streaks when everything seems to drop in for a hit, and when their success just seems to come easily. Then there are other times when a series of events keeps them from getting on base, or they miss their given target by a quarter-inch. There are days when they show up to the park and they just know things are going to go well, and other days when they "just aren't feeling it." But sometimes, in spite of the early feeling, things don't quite work out the way in which they seemed pre-destined.

For baseball pitchers, tossing a no-hitter is one of the pinnacle accomplishments in a career. At this writing, there have been just over 260 no-hitters achieved by a single pitcher (no relief pitchers) in a Major League Baseball game. There have been a number of other occasions in which more than one pitcher combined to deprive the opposing team of a hit for the duration of the game. Each of these pitchers obviously has above-average talent, but a feat of this magnitude takes a little good fortune, too.

On many occasions, the pitcher who tosses a no-hitter will comment after the game about how poorly the warm-up went. They felt a little weak and out-of-sorts, they report. And yet, when the game began, things just lined up for them.

Dock Ellis, a pitcher for the Pittsburgh Pirates and four other teams in the 1960s and 70s, reported some years later that he threw his no-hitter for the Pirates on June 12, 1970 under the influence of hallucinogenic drugs. "I was psyched. I had a feeling of euphoria. I was zeroed in on the glove but I didn't hit the glove too much. I remember hitting a couple of batters and the bases were loaded two or three times," Ellis told Bob Smizik of the Pittsburgh Post Gazette (published April 8, 1984).

Hardly the sort of approach anyone could recommend. But in spite of it, he is forever "in the club" of no-hit pitchers for his performance that day.

Some from the more select club of no-hit pitchers, who weren't on drugs, say their perceived weakness early on allowed them to focus on the few things they felt they could rely upon. Because of their perceived deficiencies, they never considered over-throwing the ball too much. Along the way, a couple of hitters helped them out by swinging at some ill-advised pitches. Then, one inning led to another, and pretty soon they found themselves staring down history.

While we're on the subject, take the case of Jim Abbott. He twirled a no-hitter while pitching for the New York Yankees against the Cleveland Indians on September 4, 1993.

If you know nothing more about baseball, that is merely an interesting footnote. However, Jim Abbott's feat is particularly amazing because he is the only man to pitch a no-hitter in the major leagues with only one hand. In fact, he is the only one-handed man to pitch at all in the history of the major leagues. Abbott's fate was to be born without a hand on the end of his right arm, but he did not accept his fate as it was presented.

That he played baseball at all, and excelled (he had prominent achievements at every level he played, including serving as the winning pitcher in the final game for the United States' first Olympic gold medal in baseball), would be enough for many people to tag him as great—and a little "lucky." But on a hazy September day in 1993, he took it to the next plateau.

Abbott started his pursuit of baseball as a child, throwing a ball against the wall and learning to transfer his glove onto his hand in time to catch it, and then transferring it again to pull the ball out of the glove and throw again. Over and over and over.

Abbott went on to play professionally for the California Angels, the New York Yankees, the Chicago White Sox, and the Milwaukee Brewers from 1989 to 1999, resting his glove on the stump of his right wrist while he threw the ball with his left hand and quickly returned his throwing hand into his glove (hopefully) before a major league hitter sent a line-drive screaming past his ear.

Once he caught the ball, he would then secure the mitt between his right forearm and torso, slip his hand out of the mitt, remove the ball from the mitt, and throw it to the appropriate base. Of course, baseball is a cruel game, and many teams attempted to bunt while Abbott was pitching (including the Cleveland Indians in the final inning of his no-hit performance), but the tactic never proved inordinately successful. One time, pitching for the U.S. in the Pan American Games, a team from Central America bunted with their first nine batters. The first man reached base. The next eight did not, and the team returned to swinging away.

Abbott is not the only one-handed player in major league history. There was Pete Gray, the one-armed outfielder for the St. Louis Browns in 1945. "I didn't grow up wanting to be another Pete Gray," said Abbott to the New York Times in 1992. "I grew up wanting to be another Nolan Ryan."

"I just don't think all of this about me playing with one hand is as big an issue as everyone wants to make it," said Abbott. "I don't try to run from the attention about it, I just accept it."

He didn't let his fortune at the end of his right arm consume him. He just loved to play baseball. He always downplayed the notion that he took satisfaction from proving people wrong about his abilities, but he did create several opportunities in his career to say to the world, "See, I told you I could!" Tempting though it might have been, he never did that.

For a period of time, Abbott was as effective as most of the pitchers of his era. But the culmination of his mastery had to be his no-hitter, even though it came at a point in his career when he began doubting his abilities. Certainly, he was lucky along the way to have a family and support structure to allow him to push on and pursue his opportunities. But getting to the stage was not enough. Abbott found a way to shine one day in September of 1993 in a manner that would parlay his good fortune into the history books.

While it is fascinating that Abbott was able to pitch at all at the major-league level (he amassed an 87-108 record during his eleven seasons, even recording a couple of base hits during his time in the National League, where pitchers have to hit for themselves), throwing a no-hitter in the heat of a pennant race seems like only a fantasy. For the event to happen in the middle of a rough patch of a mediocre year of pitching (Abbott would turn in an 11-14 record by the end of the 1993 season) seems somewhat incongruous.

Given all of the skills that he had to develop in his ascent into Major League Baseball, Abbott should never have to worry about people calling his no-hitter "lucky." But, like everyone who has accomplished the feat, he was certainly escorted by luck on this day.

His feat seems a bit more amazing when you look at the Cleveland Indians' lineup Abbott mowed through to achieve the no-no. Albert Belle, a young Manny Ramirez, Jim Thome, Kenny Lofton, and Carlos Baerga were the pin-up boys for a Cleveland lineup Abbott faced that day. The Indians had six players batting .298 or better. What's more, just five days earlier, Abbott had been shelled for seven runs in just over three innings in a start against the same team—the Indians.

So how could the winds of fate shift direction so dramatically? Tom Verducci for Sports Illustrated described a little about Abbott's pregame ritual. *"Abbott had arrived for his start wearing his lucky pair of jeans—they are marked with an X inside the waistband—and as usual, his game jersey was hanging in his locker already buttoned. It is one of the few concessions he allows for his disability; that way he can simply pull the jersey over his head."*

September 13, 1993, "A Special Delivery: That was no ordinary no-hitter Yankee Jim Abbott threw against the Indians," Tom Verducci, **Sports Illustrated**

With all of his good luck charms in place, the 25-year-old pitcher still needed a lot of things to go right that day.

Abbott's Saturday afternoon start followed a Friday night game between the two teams. Particularly toward the end of the season, this meant the manager was looking for a way to rest some of his veteran stars. A trio of players who had battered Abbott five days earlier was not in the starting lineup for this game. Still, it was a formidable group set to face the tall lefty.

Abbott's first pitch of the afternoon gave no indication of the heroics to come. Before some 30,000 fans in attendance, he yanked a fastball wide right. On a day he would never forget, he whipped his first pitch past the batter, past the catcher, and on two hops to the backstop. It was the first of two wild pitches he would uncork on the day. Additionally, he walked five batters, belying the fact that his work in this outing would go into the record books. But a date with destiny would not be deterred.

In the seventh inning, his third baseman, Wade Boggs (who had eaten his chicken dinner prior to the game), made a great defensive play on Belle, sliding to his left to swoop up a firm chopper that could have been a hit and turned it into an out by rifling a good throw over to first.

When the team returned to the dugout in the later innings, people started avoiding Abbott. It's another superstition in baseball that once a pitcher is rounding the corner toward a no-hitter, nobody on his own team wants to talk to him, for fear of jinxing what is about to unfold. So Abbott sat quietly on a lonely corner of the bench, finished the water in his cup and stacked it on top of the other cups he had emptied, one for each inning he successfully completed. Stacking cups was one of his enduring superstitions, with or without a no-hitter in play. He hadn't made many tall stacks in 1993, but on this particular day, the stack was growing.

Then, in the ninth inning, Lofton (who was one of the fastest players in baseball at the time) led off the inning by shortening to bunt on Abbott's first pitch. He fouled it down the third-base line, and drew some hearty boos from the New York Yankee fans, upon whom the historical significance of the moment was not lost. Lofton ended up hitting a chopper to the second baseman for the first of three outs Abbott needed in the ninth inning.

Upon reflection, it might have been a lucky thing that Lofton fouled off his bunt attempt instead of being the guy forever known as the person who stole a no-hitter from a one-armed pitcher by bunting with a four-run deficit.

Next came Felix Fermin. Fermin made solid contact on a strike and drove the ball to left center. Yankee center fielder Bernie Williams, who hadn't had a lot of action all day, sprinted toward the wall in left-center field to snag the curling fly ball in the air, marking the second out of the inning.

By the time Yankee shortstop Randy Velarde had fielded a grounder from Baerga at short and threw him out to end the game, history (and perhaps luck?) had come together for Jim Abbott, just as it had for scores of pitchers before him.

Was Abbott's performance lucky? Was it all part of God's plan for him? Was it karma, which rewarded him for a lifetime of achieving beyond anybody's expectations? Or did the circumstances just come together to allow his plentiful talents to shine?

"I never expected to throw a no-hitter," Abbott said in his post-game interview. "I just said (to myself), throw strikes, trust in the target, and let things fall where they may." And history happened.

Perhaps throwing a no-hitter in baseball is as much a case of not trying to impose the pitcher's will, but rather simply performing the physical task, and letting karma work with the natural abilities of everyone involved to bring home a lifetime achievement. Instead of driving the moment into history, pitchers often find themselves almost disbelieving passengers on the road to the record books. And nearly each of them recognize they were pretty fortunate on one or more occasions during the game where one of their teammates made a great play to keep the no-hitter intact.

Conversely, there are days when an athlete comes to work and feels great, but when they get into the competition, the ball bounces the wrong way, an official makes a ruling that goes against them, and pretty soon, it has turned into a terrible day at work. So what force is at play that gives us either inescapable bad luck or unbelievable good luck? The only earthly thing we can point to is our own reactions to the circumstances that arise.

A referee's bad call can get an athlete to obsess on the injustice inflicted upon them. A second close call that goes against the athlete becomes a trend (or a vendetta on behalf of the official) and now you are competing against both your opponent and the referees.

Athletes generally have pretty big egos, and to think that someone would be out to derail them is never far from their minds. Very few people can overcome this competition from the other team, the referees, and their own heads simultaneously.

Then the ball takes a bad bounce, and in the course of processing these results in the back of the mind, the athlete makes a bone-headed play. For many athletes, the solution to this series of events is to try harder to restore order. Often, rather than rectifying the situation, that precipitates more errors.

All of that can result in a cumulatively bad day.

Even without world-class athletic ability, each of us has likely been in "the zone" in some aspect of our lives. It happens on some days when everything just comes up roses. Free parking, flowers from our spouse or significant other (hopefully not on the same day), or a winning experience at the casino can all come together for a "green light day." But can this really happen to the same person who has just come off a string of really unfortunate developments? Apparently, in Jim Abbott's case, it did. Many people pass off a spate of good or bad luck as merely the "law of averages," but there may be more to it than that.

Maybe it is simply the result of being in the right place at the right time. Then, when a couple of things in a row produce a favorable result for us, we change our outlook. We begin to look for the fortunate breaks, sometimes we are able to veer around slowing traffic and continue motoring along without delay. While we are in "the zone," we see any setback as a mere speed bump on the road to where we are headed. Is being in "the zone" simply the result of changing our own outlook? Can the same be said about "bad days" that come our way? A couple of chance misfortunes, and pretty soon we are expecting that anything bad that can happen, will.

REFLECTION QUESTIONS

Is it by grand design that the rough days, when we can't seem to buy a break, really just prepare us for the times when things start falling into our laps?

Or are there other forces at work that rendezvous to create these swings of luck, one way or the other?

Was Jim Abbott lucky, or good, or both?

CHAPTER 10

THE LUCKY FORCES OUTSIDE OF US

"I never blame myself when I'm not hitting. I just blame the bat, and if it keeps up, I change bats. After all, if I know it isn't my fault that I'm not hitting, how can I get mad at myself?"

— Yogi Berra

OUR LUCK IN GAMES OF CHANCE

"Since the beginning of time there have been people who see themselves as being above the law. To them the laws don't apply. These people often hold positions in government and in the corporate world. Does a similar mentality exist within the casino world?

You betcha!"

— **John-Talmage Mathis,**
I Deal to Plunder - A ride through the boom town

As I thought about the subject of luck, it didn't take long for my mind to turn toward the many opportunities we have to call luck into our lives. Our 21st century society is riddled with ready way-stations for luck in the many gambling halls, race tracks, keno parlors, and sports books around the world. You don't even have to leave the house any more to engage in an online gambling endeavor.

Many sports begin with a flip of a coin to determine who will receive the kickoff or bat first. Indeed, in the off-chance that a local or organizational election should end in a tie, many entities are instructed through the stated rules to break the tie with a flip of the coin (oh, democracy!). It doesn't take long to develop a philosophy about this miniature game of chance. For me, I have found that if the person flipping the coin intends to catch it and flop it onto the back of their hand, you should choose the side which is face up when they flip it. If they allow the coin to fall to the ground, choose the opposite side.

Honestly, I think my odds of guessing "heads-or-tails" correctly using that philosophy of probability still stands right around 50 percent. But I feel better that I have a system, and when it works, I try to use that as the beginning of a streak of good fortune that can carry me through the game.

Perhaps it is in a gambler's mind that the fickle nature of luck is most courted. "Luck be a lady, tonight," implored Frank Sinatra in a song first performed by Marlon Brando as part of the "Guys and Dolls" musical. Stand around a craps table and watch as each thrower of the dice goes through their own unique ritual. Listen to the black jack participants as they try to keep track of their situation with the cards, pay attention to who is playing third base (directly to the dealer's right), and trying to figure out whether the current "shoe" full of cards is going to smile on the dealer, or the customers around the table. When a new deck or "shoe" of cards is brought into play, one of the players is asked to cut the cards before play begins. "Thin to win" is often uttered by the player who takes only a dozen or so card off the top of the six-deck stack, hoping for a positive result for himself and the other players at the table.

Others stalk the slot machine floor to determine where the action seems to be. Some people have even attempted to detect the harmonic differences of machines ready to pay, and those eager to take your money.

Thousands of people will take their hard-earned money and go to a casino this week, hoping that they are going to be lucky enough to parlay their earnings into something more.

It is the ultimate chance for all of us to put our money where our luck is. It is a thrill to win a little bit. It is humbling to lose it all. Ultimately, the casinos depend on the public's miscalculation of their odds. Most people look at their odds from a linear perspective. There are only fifty-two cards (not including jokers) in a standard deck of cards, and sixteen of them are either a "10" or a face card. Therefore, you have a four-in-thirteen chance of seeing one of these cards when the next one is turned over. Seems simple enough.

But which cards have already been dealt from the deck? How do multiple decks change the calculation? With the prime unknown factor of just how the cards in any particular deck shuffled into position, the linear odds become quickly inadequate to describe your chances of winning. When you go to the slot machines, things get even more complicated because the casino owners can adjust the magnets on their machines to be more or less generous from night to night. So you have three, or five, or seven wheels with a certain number of possible results, and a casino boss deciding how often the machine will stop on "Lucky 7s."

Of course, the casino operators don't want you to worry yourself about what is going on behind the curtain. They are focusing many of their efforts at marketing your luck back to you. Rarely will you see an advertisement for a casino without the vision of someone hitting it big and celebrating their good luck on the night.

Of course, as a business proposition, the casinos have to do what they can to assure that, on a macro level, the House is going to win almost every night. But while the House always wins in the aggregate, every night some individuals are going to walk out with more money than they came in with. Is it because of the "mojo" they came into the casino with, or is it simply the law of averages and their ability to sit down at the right slot machine just before it is ready to pay off?

What is interesting is that in each corner of the gambling world, the people behind the business model seem to completely discount the role of luck. The sports bookies will tell you that they have a very scientific formula for delivering more winners than losers. They are buried in statistics (many create their own formulas) for determining the point spread and how a given game may turn out in the week ahead.

But when the running back simply loses his grip on the football and fumbles the ball through the end zone, instead of scoring and covering the spread, how can you account for that? Of course, there have been athletes through the years who have been involved in point-shaving scandals, often at the encouragement of these gambling interests. It's still hard to believe "the fix is in" across-the-board in all sports—other than professional wrestling.

Attempts to influence a player's performance to the benefit of a particular betting interest is only really worth the risk, I would suppose, on the high-traffic betting games. Maybe someone would be betting on the point spread between Peru State and Concordia in men's basketball, but it would hardly be worth a "fix." Anyone who is betting on a game like this in the first place really needs to pull in at the tollbooth of life and ask him- or herself, "Have I gone too far as a degenerate gambler yet?"

The first step to a cure is admitting the addiction.

What's more, it becomes terribly obvious if someone bets $10,000 on a low-profile game, and then their best friend on the team misses all of his free throws in the fourth quarter to keep the game within the point spread.

Team sports make it incrementally more difficult to influence the outcome of a game. Unless multiple players (and maybe a coach) are involved, it can be difficult to create a favorable betting proposition for the game beforehand. And even then, the coaches and players still have to execute the plan to make a whole lot of people "lucky" with point spread magic. You can't be too obvious when you are rolling over. It has to look like "just one of those days" to the rest of the world.

Mischief of this sort would reasonably be attracted to a game that has a high degree of interest. In many ways, casinos have understood this high-traffic relationship. Most high-level casinos and resorts make their gaming floors places where people want to be. As the casino owners have renovated over the past twenty years, they have attached impressive performance halls, restaurants, and auditoriums to provide entertainment within a close proximity of the gambling floor. Each night, the House can set the payout percentage for their many millions of slot machines across the world.

Allen Moody, in his first book, *Becoming a Winning Gambler*, actually looks at gambling from the perspective of playing only those games where luck isn't as large of a factor...blackjack, horse racing, poker, and sports betting. "Some could argue that the New York Jets covering the point spread was lucky, or they had a lucky run of cards at the tables, but again, I always refer to probability and laws of averages," he says.

Moody continues by offering an example. "A woman recently won the SuperContest (football pick 'em game) of roughly $447,000 and was close to picking 64 percent of her games against the spread correctly, which is pretty impressive. Some people, possibly even herself, would say she was lucky to attain that percentage. I would take the point of view that in a contest with 600 people, the law of averages say that somebody is going to obtain a percentage near that, just as if you flipped a coin 100 times and did it 600 different times, you would no doubt have runs where there were 61 tails and 39 heads or 58 heads and 42 tails, etc."

Surely, in that same contest, someone only picked 36 percent of the winners. Their performance went relatively unnoticed, except by their spouse if they were betting the rent money.

It seems to be a common refrain from the owners of the gaming community. It is *not* a game from their perspective, but rather a cold calculation of the odds and probabilities that assures their business will continue. Done right, any $1,000 winner is only taking a small portion of the money other people have lost on that given night.

Indeed, there have been groups of people who have discovered how to count cards, or influence jockeys, or sense the buzz of a machine ready to pay. Like all people who deal in luck, they are looking for a system or a pattern that will help them perform better than the game that is stacked against them says they should. But people who suddenly appear to be excessively lucky only raise the suspicions of the gaming parlor operators. If you are a regular winner, someone from the casino will likely want to talk with you. They will be very interested in how you are winning, if they have not already been able to decipher your system from the array of cameras posted throughout the facility.

"How are you doing it?" is a natural question we'd all like to know. Most of us would like to ride that golden goose for awhile. The casino owners would like to smother the goose, and all of its kin.

Some could argue that the silver dollar in their pocket, or the rabbit's foot, or the good karma from the rest of the people at the table, played a role in the night's outcome in the gambling hall. But that is very rarely the lone source of winning, night after night. Casino operators are presented with a regular stream of "winners" who can be shown in the advertisements to other gamblers who have yet to come to the casino with the "loosest slots." But the same person rarely shows up on their advertisements over and over again. You might be more likely to see those perpetual winners on "Wanted" posters at the post office, and certainly on the "Not Invited" list at the casinos.

Of course, the losers just get in their cars (if they stopped gambling before they had to sell their car to pay their debt) and go home. There are not a lot of attractive stories about those of us who lose. They are certainly not the stories the casinos want to show in order to attract future customers.

Although it stands as an accepted fact that overall the odds are against us, every night someone still walks out of the casino with a little more money than they came in with. After all, the casinos can't maintain their business by taking everyone's money all the time. Someone has to occasionally screech in delight at a big win. Tonight, it might be you who feels lucky.

The casino operators, however, do not consider you as lucky, even though they will appeal to your "lucky side" in their marketing campaigns. If you happen to sit down in front of a machine that is mechanically ready to pay out, you will benefit. If not, you will scrape along and, on average, come out a little bit behind. Which day, and what time you arrive, and what game you choose has a very real impact on whether you will have good luck or bad luck.

Having once won on the "Wizard of Oz," machine, a player may circle that area of the casino on their next visit (even the next night), sure that their karma is in alignment with that machine. When the chair becomes available, however, chances are very good that the machine is not in the same pay-out cycle as it was before.

And even if the mechanical odds say we should get between 95 and 98 percent of our gambling investment back, when we allow our hearts and hunches to play into the equation, the odds for the House increase. It's all enough to entice some of us beyond our willpower to stop when we are a little ahead, or to stay with the percentages.

There is nothing like a big win to get the emotional excitement roiling, which usually causes us to abandon the cold, hard rules of the game. Once we start "playing with the House's money," it is tempting to throw caution to the wind. At which point the odds swing decidedly the House's way.

Even accepting the notion that the House is set up to win, there is still the matter about the minority of us common gamblers who, tonight at least, will not lose. The people who will tell you they win more than they lose on a regular basis, all believe they have a system in place—even if they are just kidding themselves. Most of the time, these people suffer from selective amnesia, but if you can get a gambler's attention at the bar, ask them about their rituals of luck. Most of them are happy to share what they think they know—unless they think talking about such things will negate their lucky streak.

Depending on the game, the variations on summoning luck are vast. In craps, some people blow on the dice (or have their neighbor blow for them). Some people put the dice in a particular configuration before they pick them up from the table. Some people throw the dice with their hand above the dice, and some throw them with their hands under the dice, and some throw then with a little twist of the wrist. The rituals are so involved that you begin to believe there might be something to it. Until the "shooter" craps out, then we have to build the cone of luck all over again with a new roller.

Many people play the card games, because they believe the human involvement makes it less a matter of sheer luck, especially in poker and blackjack. The cards still come up in an assumedly random order. The randomness of a 52-card deck (or six) is the ultimate arbiter on whatever "system" you might work out. Some Harvard boys with incredible memories and a quantum equation in their heads figured something out at the Las Vegas blackjack table a few years back, but they are not warmly welcomed by the casinos anymore.

The essence of their theory was watching for the number of 10-count cards that come out of the shoe early. If a lot of smaller cards come out first, the odds turn to favor the customer. If the 10s, Jacks, Queens, and Kings come out early, the odds swing toward the House. This is not a lead-pipe-certain theory, and with six decks in the shoe, there are always a few 10-count cards to spoil the stew, but that is the essence of the theory.

As I have played blackjack, I have noticed it is common to double your bet immediately after the dealer deals him/herself a 21. According to theory, minus the cards you have already seen, the chances are about the same for the dealer to take everyone's money in the next hand, but often it just feels right to chase good money after bad. It often turns out as dumb as it seems on the surface. When it works, though, it's magic.

In my experience, it is always good to look for a veteran blackjack player sitting at "third base," directly to the dealer's right. "Third base" is an important position at the table because that person gets to choose whether to take one more card immediately before the dealer gets some. If the person at "third base" has some sense of the cards already played, and those remaining in the deck, everyone's odds rise slightly. Of course, people sitting at any position at the table can take too many cards when they shouldn't. But when I'm looking for a good table, I start from the dealer and work my way around counter-clockwise.

There are, of course, always several cards in the deck on which the dealer can win, and in a random deck, they are always subject to flipping face up at just the right time to ruin the moment. This recurring theme is one reason I haven't struck it rich in the casinos. I attempt to salvage my pride by assuring myself that I just gamble for the recreation. If you are in it to have more money on the table than you can afford to lose (there is a masochistic buzz to that drama), it is generally time to stop playing and find another hobby.

Like every ritual or superstition, the ones employed by gamblers offer no guarantees to success. The slot machine that paid out big money yesterday is an inanimate object. It is not capable of developing a fond affection for you, so you would be well-advised to keep moving. Perhaps the "ready-to-pay" machine is on the other side of the gambling floor today.

Therefore, if you do take an occasional trip to the riverboat, it remains a great idea to only bet the money you can afford to lose. If you are using money that should be paying another bill, you are putting way too much stock in luck, or your "system" to outdistance luck's return.

Many have tried it, and very few who started poor became rich by gambling. Play until you have lost a predetermined amount, then go home.

One of the luckiest characteristics a gambler can possess is knowing when to cash in and go home. Untold fortunes have been lost by gamblers who, in one moment, won a modest-sized pot, but then got greedy (thinking their luck was turning) and began betting wildly with their fortuitous gains.

After all, you can never really score a big win, unless you bet some big money. So you are often tempted to drop your winnings on one final spin of the wheel. You might parlay your winnings into an outrageous fortune, or chances are, you will surrender all you have gained and walk away shaking your head.

As Kenny Rogers reminded us incessantly during the 1970s and 1980s, "*You've got to know when to hold them, and know when to fold them. Know when to walk away. Know when to run.*" I don't suppose his song would've gotten as much airtime on the radio over the past forty years, if it weren't so patently true at its core. Your best chance of winning during your next trip to the casino comes in knowing when to leave. Hands down.

For those of us who like our money too much to be chronic gamblers, the standard game of Klondike solitaire provides us an economical way to play with luck. Writers waiting for just the right inspiration play many hundreds of games of solitaire (at least this one has), and the computer makes playing and tracking your success much easier.

If you are playing well and paying attention to each game without cheating, you might do well enough to win about 18 percent of the time. Indeed, in casinos where they allow you to play solitaire for money, you buy the cards for a dollar apiece, and receive $5 back for every card you are able to "put up." Thus, you need to get eleven cards up in a game to make a profit. So the "18 percent" axiom is one the casinos believe as well. Yes, you might win three out of four games on some "lucky" days, but you will also find a rough patch where you lose fifteen in a row. Generally, the random nature of the cards will come to find you over time, regardless of the theories or strategies you employ.

The cards, the dice, the spinning wheels of roulette, or the slot machines provide different mediums of randomness, but they are all calculated (or adjusted mechanically) to beat us in the end. If you are fortunate enough to capture a streak of good luck, the most important thing to remember is to keep your perspective. Quit in time to carry that winning feeling around with you for awhile. It is a mirage, but it feels good for the rest of the night after you were "in the right place at the right time."

REFLECTION QUESTIONS

How much of a role do you believe luck plays at the casino?

Are some people luckier than others?

What are your lucky rituals in games of chance?

LUCKY IN WAR?

"He has been pursued, day by day and year by year, by a most phenomenal and astonishing luckiness. He has been a shining soldier in all our wars for a generation; he has littered his whole military life with blunders, and yet has never committed one that didn't make him a knight or a baronet or a lord or something. Look at his breast; why, he is just clothed in domestic and foreign decorations. Well, sir, every one of them is the record of some shouting stupidity or other; and taken together, they are proof that the very best thing in all this world that can befall a man is to be born lucky."

"Luck," by Mark Twain
http://www.classicshorts.com/stories/luck.html

Throughout the history of mankind, whenever we have been faced with the most dire of outlooks, we will grasp at any possibility for deliverance from the ordeal. Whether it is dumb luck or divine intervention, we will accept any indication that gives us hope.

During the Middle Ages, people asked for luck in escaping the fatal grasp of the Yellow Fever, or The Plague, or Malaria. They also asked for luck in resisting or averting wandering hordes of armies moving across the landscape. In the early 21st century, many people are praying for a cure for cancer in any of its unforgiving forms. If you've ever had a child or a sibling with some form of disability, you have probably experienced first-hand the desperate search for answers that often seem futilely elusive. And so it continues.

For the able-bodied among us, there is still no more poignant example of the search for a twist of good luck than in a time of war. Through nearly every age, human civilizations have seen fit to send a significant portion of our populace into the hellish theater of war to "advance" our society's goals. Whether it is a war to support ideology (capitalism over communism, Christianity over Islam, freedom over oppression), executing the role as the world's police officer (to right a world's wrong), or sheer imperialism (to gain control of natural resources), the fundamental nature of war has remained the same. We cast our young people unto the battlefield, where opposing forces are actively trying to kill them.

In a heated war scenario, all manner of projectiles are hurtling back and forth. These weapons are cast about, ricocheting off trees, buildings, and even the ground in a terrifying curtain of destruction.

In such situations where an individual has so little control, it is human nature to grasp for any comfort we can find. Of course, military training attempts to stress the importance of being prepared for a wide array of eventualities, but war often includes unpredictable moments of chaos.

After all, without a little bit of luck, our little colonial revolution against the King of England might have been squashed as soon as it began in 1776.

A month after the signing of the Declaration of Independence, a group of maybe 10,000 colonials had dug in around New York City. Novices in war and bursting with pride, the rag-tag colonial army under General George Washington's command had no idea how outmanned they were against the English military force numbering nearly 40,000 men and a vast armada of naval strength. For the most part, the Americans had rowboats and merchant ships for a Navy.

The revolutionaries soon found out how unprepared they were in both equipment and in courage. War was really not as glorious as it seemed when these farmers and tradesman signed up to be soldiers.

In David McCullough's book, *John Adams*, the scene was described starkly.

> *"The inexperienced Americans were outnumbered, out-flanked, and overwhelmed in only a few hours. Most had never been in battle, and while many fought hard and courageously, many did not . . . More than 1,000 Americans were captured, wounded, or killed, and among the prisoners were several generals."*
>
> (page 151-152)

Whatever forces the colonials were calling on for good luck, luck was not going to be enough to overcome this force face-to-face. Things went so poorly for the prospective Americans that the entire force could have been snuffed out there and then, except for a timely storm with an accompanying north wind, which kept the British from sailing their vast armada up the East River and finishing the skirmish in decisive fashion.

This fateful meteorological development allowed Washington an escape route, and his forces were able to regroup and reinforce within the vastness of the mainland and to buy time to choose more favorable future engagements.

For that, the entire dream of a free United States of America should consider itself lucky.

Of course, that was not the only good fortune the American military has encountered. The stories about the weather and tides surrounding the D-Day invasion of France in World War II are legendary. The Allies' success on that blustery day played a significant role in the eventual demise of the Third Reich and Adolf Hitler's dream of conquering the world.

A stormy day on the French coastline would create many complications for the forces. As it was, the weather was borderline. The waves were choppy, and that influenced how close to the shore the invasion forces could get before they unleashed the tanks and troops necessary. In some locations, the tanks were rendered useless because they were launched too far away from the shore. The density of the sand was also an issue in moving heavy equipment.

So many plans go into a successful invasion, and so many factors could have changed the course of events.

While luck becomes a more complex consideration for an entire expeditionary force, individuals going into the battle each hold their own set of rituals, which they believe improve their chances of surviving their next military encounter.

We've heard the story of the Army private whose dog tags hanging around his neck stopped a bullet from piercing his heart, rendering the weird-looking necklace to the esteemed lifelong position of "lucky charm" on that soldier's dressing table. But are there other pleas for luck used by the unfortunate young men who are sent into harm's way by pompous old men through the years?

"It's true that in a foxhole, nobody is an atheist," says Vietnam veteran Jerry McFarland, who served in the Army's 403rd Special Operations Detachment. "If you are getting shot at or shelled, luck is the least of your concerns. You are in survival mode. You are not counting on luck, you are counting on your training."

"Before going to battle, I suppose, everyone has their rituals," he admits. "And afterward, you get time to reflect on the 'what-ifs.' But during the heat of the battle, you are doing what you are trained to do to stay alive."

"If a soldier always puts his left boot on first prior to going to battle, are they doing that as part of their luck ritual, or is it simply a mechanism of getting prepared?" McFarland asks. "If something particularly fortunate happened while you were wearing a certain set of fatigues, you might make it a point to wear those the next time you anticipate trouble."

"It's kind of like a batter fidgeting with his batting gloves between pitches, the rituals help get his or her mind in the right place so they can feel prepared," McFarland adds. The difference between sports and war can be illustrated by the fact that, if a batter falls into a slump, he may well get a new pair of batting gloves. If a soldier has a string of negative outcomes, he may not get a chance to change his socks.

After a soldier emerges from combat, McFarland says, they often come home wondering "what-if" they had done certain things differently. For him, his thoughts have often turned to a fellow soldier in his unit, who was killed because he chose to go on a unique path, instead of following Jerry along his route.

"If I had grabbed him and pulled him along beside me, or if I would have gone with him, he might still be alive today." Both Jerry and his dead fellow soldier, it turns out, were both unlucky that he didn't force his fresh-faced buddy down the safer trail. His buddy's luck was sudden and certain. Jerry has carried his burden for decades.

Jerry also points to the case of his buddy Robert K. Stevens, who was lucky that his Vietnam War assignment was to work in the water treatment plant for the Air Force. "He was placed as far away from the fighting as he could get," Jerry recalls. "He was in a secured facility. He wore a clean uniform every day. He slept in an air-conditioned bunk."

But the Viet Cong did not consider anything off limits. So one day, when Stevens was "herding turds," the water treatment facility was hit with a white phosphorus grenade. The blast, and subsequent chemical reaction melted his face away, burned his legs, and reduced the fingers on his hands to just a few nubs. Since that fateful day, Stevens has had hundreds of rounds of plastic surgery, which restored his body to some degree of function. Returning to civilian life, Stevens came to enjoy fishing and hunting, and even opened his own bait and tackle shop. As the result of his injuries, the government continued to send him a nice monthly check.

"Stevens never really worked a day in his life that he didn't want to," Jerry says. "Of course, he went through things none of us can even imagine, but in the end, things turned out better for him than it did for many other people."

He bore a terrible burden for his service, but could Robert K. Stevens ever consider himself lucky?

Ryan Glasco served two tours of duty totaling twenty-six months in Afghanistan with the 173rd Airborne brigade of the U.S. Army. In all, he served in uniform for eight years, and was wounded by friendly fire in his last trip to Afghanistan.

Ryan agrees that, when in the middle of a battle, training trumps luck. "Our training really instills a sense of preparation and muscle memory. We all have to be able to anticipate the actions of our fellow soldiers, and that's why our training really is the most important element of combat."

But right up to the point of confrontation, there are numerous ways soldiers try to get their lucky stars aligned.

"I had a little medallion that I wore around my neck," Ryan says. "It was on the same chain as my dog tags. I always rubbed that between my thumb and forefinger. In the barracks, getting ready to head out, even in the HumVee on patrol, rubbing that medallion gave me some comfort. Once the bullets started flying, though, it's all business."

As a group, his battle team also had rituals. They always prayed to St. Michael, the patron saint of the airborne infantry. Many subgroups of the military have adopted patron saints to look over them. This is probably a bow in the direction of divine intervention, but for many it was a small bow in the direction of "just in case."

"Like most of the people on my team, I am not Catholic, but we all said a prayer for St. Michael to watch over us," Ryan says. "If there really is someone in Heaven assigned to be on your side, we all just felt it was a pretty good idea to show our appreciation."

Not all rituals had religious overtones. "We had one guy who smoked a cigar before every mission," Ryan says. "That was his thing."

Ryan also described the practices of placing a name tape, with the name of a loved one on it, inside your clothing so as not to interfere with the regulation appearance the Army demands. Many soldiers also weave an extra set of dog tags in with their bootlaces. Another practice is to write your blood type on the back of your boots, or in some other inconspicuous location.

"Those things started long ago, maybe with some functional purpose, but now they are merely done out of tradition," Ryan says.

Circumstances surrounding war, though, often cause things to happen both rapidly and furiously. Such was the case with Ryan's eventual war wound. It was a wound he was very unlucky to receive. At the same time, there were many strokes of good fortune that helped him ultimately survive.

"One day in October 2010, we were doing a mission and we were engaged by the Taliban," he remembered. "The patrol was ambushed and the .50 caliber gun on top of our vehicle (which might ordinarily clear the bushes of trouble) jammed. We all bugged out and found cover near the vehicle. The gunner atop the vehicle worked feverishly to fix the jam. When he finally worked things loose, the gun discharged one round in my direction. I was shot in the thigh, the bullet exploded my femur damaged the vein that pushes blood back into my torso. I still suffer from peroneal nerve damage.

"Both the Platoon medic and my dismounted team leader ran through enemy fire to treat me and carry me back through that same enemy fire.

"Instead of being flown out by helicopter and being back on base in about twenty minutes to receive medical aid, I was placed in a non-armored Afghan 'medical' vehicle (with almost no medical supplies and a well-worn set of shock absorbers), where I endured a return to base that took over an hour, with the prospect of being ambushed as we returned over land. Perhaps fortunately, I was lapsing in and out of consciousness, so the trip didn't seem to take that long. Once back at base, the surgeon who stabilized me began yelling at our medic for not flying me out."

If you were trying to track the various opportunities to claim good or bad luck from Ryan's incident, you might have gotten a little dizzy. The gun jammed, which was bad luck. When it was repaired it spit out a round at him, which was further bad luck. However, why the gun only discharged one round when it was cleared, and not the entire belt's load of bullets, is a mystery that nobody can answer even today. That little development was extremely good luck, given what a lone .50-caliber shell did to his leg that day.

He was very lucky to be fighting with a cadre of brave colleagues, and he was very lucky that his return to base was not met with any further encounters with the enemy. Again, all of the American soldiers involved were merely reverting to their training and their humanity to do their job. Panic did not get in their way, and their bravery prevailed. Lucky for him.

Ryan has very much benefited from modern medical treatment that is at least advanced enough to give a person with this sort of wound a decent chance to recover. He was extremely fortunate that the bullet did not seriously compromise the arteries and veins running to and from his leg. An inch one way of the other, and he could have bled out. Even at that, the Army doctor in Germany told him that if he was ever able to walk again, he would not walk normally. Today, thanks to the miracles of modern medicine (and his own hard work in rehab), they have reconstructed his leg with rods and screws and he is walking relatively normally, and even participating in fitness tests which include running a variety of distances.

"I definitely feel pain when the weather changes," Ryan admits. "But other than that, I feel pretty close to normal."

But individual decisions along the way also have left him with lingering regrets and bitterness. He was interested in recognizing his colleagues who ultimately helped save his life. But Army politics stood in the way.

"Once I was evacuated back into the hands of medical personnel in Landstuhl, Germany, I recommended both my dismounted team leader, and the medic for bronze stars. Both were denied, along with a denial of my second purple heart, simply because the legal official said it was not friendly fire. Instead it was deemed a malfunction in a firefight, which is apparently totally different."

The men who saved his life would not be recognized by the military for their bravery.

Whether that is categorized a stroke of bad luck, or just poor judgment by the military is another quandary to ponder. But the final power of luck can only be determined by how you react to adversity. Ryan has moved on.

From the first report of his injury, many people have prayed for his recovery. And he has shown the will and determination that makes you believe he will recover, but he will never forget the story of how fate changed his life that day. But because he lived, he has more to do.

"I wouldn't have changed anything," he says in reflection. "Just because of all I had to endure afterwards, it showed me what I was made of mentally. I knew what I could do physically, but you learn a lot about yourself from a mental standpoint when you are faced with such a life-changing situation. Sitting alone in that hospital bed in Germany, a lot of things descended upon me. My world had changed."

While he could have spent all of his time thinking about the things he couldn't do, he had some other distractions. He and his girlfriend grew closer together, eventually getting married and having a beautiful daughter. Ryan left the Army, but was accepted into the Army Reserves. He continues to search for a post-military career while battling the effects of Post Traumatic Stress Disorder. Life could be better, but life could also be non-existent.

Because Ryan was lucky enough to live through the life-and-death situation he faced in Afghanistan, who among us could tell him that rubbing that metal medallion of his wasn't the deciding factor? And if St. Michael was the deciding factor in whether he (and many other airborne infantry personnel) would live or die, all praise to him.

A lot of people have told Ryan he is very lucky since he returned from Afghanistan. And he is. But his "luck" comes at a price many of us would not care to pay just to boast about our good fortune.

Living and breathing in the "trenches" of war may provide us with some of the most dramatic pleas for luck, but there are many thousands of military personnel who serve this country in other less-harrowing ways.

Since World War II, America's sailors serving in the Navy have rarely faced a direct combat threat, other than a few terrorist attacks such as the one against USS Cole. Since mastering the art of war with aircraft carriers, the primary role of our Navy has been to provide offshore support to ground-based military actions (I know, the Marines are the boots-on-the-ground arm of the Navy, and there are many stories that, no doubt, parallel those of the Army men discussed above).

Still, there are many dangerous jobs in the Navy. Perhaps none as patently dangerous as catching and catapulting planes on the deck of an aircraft carrier.

Dave Michener served in the U.S. Navy from 1986 to 1992. He entered the Navy out of high school, aspiring to enter as a photographer's mate. Like many pursuits in the Navy, there is a training school for young sailors to obtain basic training for this assignment.

"I did really well on all of the (physical) performance tests," he says. "But when it came to the tests we had to study for, I didn't do so well." His aversion to studying, which delivered less-than-stellar results in high school, was one of the reasons he went into the Navy (besides following in the footsteps of his father and his grandfather). In the Navy, if you fail just one class, you are expelled from the specialists training.

When the academic training doesn't work out, the Navy sends the budding sailors into active duty as an "undesignated seaman." This generally means you can be assigned a wide array of duties that do not require special training, which can range from scraping barnacles off the side of the ship, to laundry detail, or working in the engine room.

Initially, Michener was assigned to the catapult and catch team on the USS Coral Sea. This group was charged with launching and catching 20-ton fighter jets (costing $65 million each) from the deck of the carrier using a cable system. Many things can go terribly wrong, especially when the ship is in "scramble" mode. It's a place where you really want to know what you are doing.

"We would have three or four catapults working at the same time," Dave remembers. "Planes are all over the place. You really have to keep your head on a swivel. Plus, on a ship, there are variables you don't have on dry land. For one, the ship is moving up and down on the waves."

While the deck of the carrier is typically 100 feet above the water line, Michener recalls several occasions when the waves lapped up over the deck. "The most dangerous jobs on the ship were often given to those with the least experience and those with the most experience," Michener notes. "It's funny now how fondly I look back on it now, but it is really amazing that I survived."

Perhaps his luckiest moment in the Navy came when he mentioned to one of his superiors that he knew how to type really well. He gained the skill in high school, when his old-school typing teacher walked up and down the aisles of the classroom with a ruler. If any of her students looked down on their keyboard, she would slap them across the wrist.

"I got a couple of bloody knuckles before I stopped looking down, but after that, I learned how to type really fast. I began to challenge myself to be the fastest in the class," he remembers. "And those skills got me off the flight deck."

His skill landed him a job tracking the records for the Aircraft Launch and Recovery Maintenance Program. Which means, basically, he went from catching jets with a wire to creating and completing databases with his computer—in a sheltered office, somewhat out of harm's way.

Before he left the Navy, the USS Coral Sea was retired and he served on the first crew aboard the USS Abraham Lincoln. His tour of duty happened during a period when the United States was not engaged in formal wartime operations. They hovered off Libya's shores for awhile when Muammar Ghadafi was supporting terrorist activities and drew the attention of American leaders. Michener and his shipmates sat off the coast of Israel "battle ready" for forty-two days when tensions rose in that part of the world. They provided support to forces in Kuwait and Iraq when hostilities arose there. They also supported rescue and relief efforts when Mount Pinatubo erupted in the Philippines.

Michener witnessed an array of rituals, superstitions, and expressions of luck among many of his 5,000 shipmates during his service. The one he most remembers is Petty Officer Paine (ironically enough) who worked on the catapult team. Paine woke up one morning with an ominous feeling something was going to happen. When he had these feelings, he always liked to wear the working clothes he wore the previous day (because nothing bad had happened yesterday). On this particular morning, his clothes from the previous day were an oily mess, but he put them on anyway. Later in the day, another member of the catapult team was focusing on a plane taxiing on the deck, and failed to notice a plane coming up behind him. This unfortunate seaman's leg was run over by the plane that came up from behind him.

"Paine always said that could have been him, if it weren't for those oily clothes he was wearing," Michener recounts. And a superstition grew in stature (at least for Petty Officer Paine).

There were other occasions, when he was off-duty, when Michener cites his luck. On shore leave in Naples, Italy, he and some ship-mates had stopped into a club to have a few beers. "I always hated to stay too long in the places that were loaded with American military," Michener remembers. "For one, you spend weeks at a time trapped on a ship with these people. I like to see the sights when I am on shore leave, instead of looking at the same group of people."

Later that day, a bomb went off in the club he had only just left. Terrorism was just getting a toehold in our consciousness in the late 1980s and early 1990s. Luckily, Michener and his small group of buddies had moved on and escaped injury in Naples. A similar situation occurred when he was in Santiago, Chile. But for the grace of God, or his karma, or just dumb luck, he was not in those club bombings, which injured many other American servicemen.

Danger is never too far afield for the people who serve in the military. Fortunately, the American armed forces train our troops to be as prepared as humanly possible. But it doesn't hurt to be just a little lucky on the side.

REFLECTION QUESTIONS

Drawing from your own experiences, or those of a friend or family member, how does fighting in a war change a person's outlook on life?

Does war change our view of luck?

LUCKY IN LOVE?

"Theirs is a great story, no question, but I couldn't get on board with her theory that fate had a hand in the matter. The way I figured it, she was probably just really, really lucky. Because if everyone is fated to have an amazing love life, wouldn't we all be dating Ryan Gosling right now?"

— **Jamie Beckman**, *The Frisky*
(Cnn.com), "Does 'lucky in love' really exist?"

"Most young women do not welcome promiscuous advances. (Either that, or my luck's terrible.)"

— **Groucho Marx**,
Memoirs Of A Mangy Lover

Because the differences between war and love are sometimes indistinguishable in our lives, it is certain that on any given day, more people are looking for the winds of good fortune to blow their way when it comes to the personal affairs of the heart. While it is a little less likely to be a life-and-death matter—such as you would find in a theater of war—there have been many instances in human existence in which the fanatical pursuit of love has ended in death. Sometimes the consequences of our pursuit of love can create a living hell that feels even worse than death. We all have to live with the carnage we create in the wake of our search for love.

Even if you engage in a one-night stand, memories endure, and sometimes other consequences result. For most of us, the indiscretion will endure in our consciences for the rest of our lives. All we need is the innocent mention of a name, or a town, or an event, and the memories (and adjoining feelings) are subject to resurfacing.

Most of us have heard of people described as being "lucky in love." The area of love is one where, once again, everyone gets to define what they consider good luck, and what they consider not-so-good. I've seen couples who are definitely creating their own definitions of what they consider good luck in their love life. From the outside, we can't always see what two people see in each other (or used to). That they have been able to find each other and create an understanding between themselves is lucky indeed. Having a true life-partner is a wonderful thing and makes a lot of things easier along our journey.

Maybe being lucky in love is as simple as not allowing the unsuccessful or unsavory turns to haunt you later in life. Or maybe people who are lucky in love have no skeletons in their closet to haunt them in the first place. Or no closet in which to keep them stored.

In college, the definition of "lucky in love" very much paralleled the definition of "getting lucky." There were certain guys who always seemed to attract the attention of the amorous females. The rest of us watched the parade (which sometimes morphed into a circus), and kept our eyes open for rebounding opportunities.

There are women and men in this world who consider themselves lucky because they are married to someone who doesn't physically abuse them. That is an admittedly low bar, but you have to recognize them for finding the silver lining in their situation. If you've ever been in (or known someone in) an abusive situation, you more easily recognize the tremendous benefits that living without abuse can provide.

But still, there are people who cannot escape the cycle of abuse. They get out of a particular relationship, but then fall back into another different, but equally demeaning, relationship. There is a lot to be said for the fact that what we each bring into a relationship determines what we will get out of it.

If you are always looking for love in a bar, the chances of finding an alcoholic for your next mate are greatly increased. It doesn't have to work that way, but there is obviously a higher proportion of drunkards in a bar than at a church supper.

The scariest proposition of human relationships is that it works best when two people can establish a common set of goals, experiences, and expectations in the relationship. The more partitions we create (be they behaviors, habits, or pursuits) to inhibit commonality ("because I say so"), the more difficult it is to incorporate two lives into a single relationship.

Sometimes that means trying something new, or allowing your partner to show you something they have experienced. Sometimes it means trying something neither of you have ever done before, which gives you a common, unique experience. It is exploring the world around us, together, that helps us to build the earthly axis on which our relationship rotates.

If you are not willing to merge your life perspectives together, realizing that one partner can be a Democrat and the other a Republican, it is difficult to fully commit your lives to one another. Sooner or later, if the differences can no longer be tolerated, they become the smoldering flashpoint for a breakup. They drown out any commonalities on which your relationship is built.

One partner's drinking habit could have been completely fine when the couple was young and on the bar circuit regularly. But once the couple begins having children, the incessant drinking isn't fun anymore. It's simply becomes a logistical barrier to raising the children as a parental team.

If you are out looking for your next partner in the bars, it is important to determine whether your prospective mate has developed an intimate (maybe exclusive) relationship with alcohol. Sometimes the relationship with booze (or drugs, or a wide array of potential addictions) is stronger than the relationship they are able to have with any human. But if the couple is comfortable operating in a threesome with drugs or alcohol, the relationship can still work. It is just a bit more perilous.

While on the macro level, love may well have more to do with our human response to a given situation, there are points of luck and fortune that all of us can point to in the budding of a new romance. How did you first meet your spouse?

I met my first wife while I was doing some political canvassing in a suburb of Denver on behalf of then-U.S. Senator Tim Wirth. It was an in-between job for a 25-year-old bachelor trying to make a little money between reporter jobs. My task was to go door-to-door handing out literature and asking for donations to the campaign. The gig didn't last too long. I was interested in talking to people, and if I collected a little money, all the better. The campaign folks really wanted the money, and if I met some interesting people along the way, so be it.

Obviously, my employer and I just didn't have the same goals.

As you walk up and down the sidewalks of middle-class America, you see a lot of interesting things. On this day, the surprise came stealthily dressed as a children's birthday party.

I rang my 10th doorbell on the day, and a middle-aged lady came to the door. I started my short declaration of who I was and why I was there. Before I got to the end of the second sentence, the lady says, "We have a kid's birthday party going on here now, and I have a bunch of adults in here at the table. Why don't you come in and talk to the group?

Well, I was there to talk to people, so I took the bait.

I went into the dining room and I started again with my short speech. At the end, I could tell pretty easily: they were underwhelmed. From the corner, one of the men in the group says, "Well, I don't care one way or the other about Tim Wirth, but I'll give you five dollars if you take Kirsten here out on a date."

The mid-20s mom next to him, turned red and kind of slumped in her chair. But before she could completely shrink into the woodwork, I said, "Sure, I'm not doing anything Saturday night."

Turns out, Kirsten had been divorced from her first husband just long enough to start wondering where her life with two young boys was going from here. After she recovered from the embarrassment of being put on the spot, she didn't put the brakes on this crude effort at matchmaking. I guess I did appear to be worth a chance in the lottery of love—scar and all.

The next thing I knew, a name was on the sheet, five dollars was in my collection satchel, and I had a date. Through circumstances I could not accurately recount now, I stayed the night with Kirsten on the night of our first date, and nearly every night after that for the next two decades. She had two young boys (ages two and three) coming into the relationship, and within a couple of years, we were married and were lucky to produce a smart and beautiful daughter between us. I am very grateful for the relationships I was able to forge with those kids while they were growing into adults. All three kids and I are still pretty close today, and as they begin producing a beautiful batch of grandchildren for my entertainment, I can see the cycle of life turning for them just as it did for me. That is both scary and exciting.

For Kirsten and me, over time our diverse levels of education, our differing interests, and the differing levels of importance we placed on sobriety separated us. So after twenty years of raising our family, we parted company—like so many other couples—in our own divorce.

So in middle age, I found myself single again. Wallowing in a little self-pity, and trying to keep a career alive (so I would have a way to continue paying child support for our daughter), I tried to identify the traits I desired in my next mate.

Before I got a good list together, back into my life came a very good friend. Serendipity came to the fore, and it was working in my favor. This time, love came knocking on *my* door. Fortunately, I let her in.

When Pam McCurdy and I first met, we were both in our teens; and, to each other, neither one of us looked like the sort of person we wanted to marry and spend the rest of our lives with. But there was an intellectual and physical attraction. She lived in Concord, California, where my parents had moved. She went to the same church as my parents, and she was the same age as my younger sisters.

Our time together was spotty and brief, mostly limited to when I would come home from college in Colorado over the holidays, summers, or on spring break. At college, I had forged a relationship with a couple of other girls over my four years. But I was very selfish, and really didn't understand much about relationships having anything to do with merging lives. How can such a stupid guy come wrapped in such a smart-looking (although slightly dented) wrapper?

During my visits to California, Pam and I started going out to dinner. We would spend time in the city park walking, talking, and sitting on the bleachers at the softball fields. We were establishing some common experiences. But opportunity never quite came together to allow us to make a longer-term commitment.

Pam married a guy she went to high school with in California. A couple of years later, I met Kirsten.

The story appeared to have run its course until I received an email in the midst of my marriage's decline nearly twenty years later. One night, Pam (living in California) was exploring the wonders of the Internet search engine, and decided to send an e-mail to a "Brian Hale" (living in Nebraska) to ask whether this was "the" Brian Hale whose family lived in California in the 1980s and 1990s.

I was intrigued by the inquiry. It seemed like an innocent question from an old friend who was 1,700 miles away, so I confirmed that I *was* the Brian Hale for which she was searching.

As it turned out, her marriage was also on the rocks. The turmoil of a troubled relationship is something I could wish on nobody. On the other hand, by some fate of the cosmos—and through different circumstances—we were becoming available for a relationship at the same time. Luckily, we were now a bit more mature and battle-wise in our 40s. And we had each changed a little over time. The traits we were looking for in a new partner now looked very similar to what each of us could bring to the table.

What's more, all of the developments in our lives happened at about the same time electronic communications made it easier for people to connect (and re-connect) with each other, no matter the geographic differences.

Subsequent developments in online dating sites, social media, and Skype has made electronic romances much more common nowadays. I know several people who are in relationships initially established by visiting and screening people online, without ever being in the same room. People have been known to represent themselves in a manner very different than how they behave. And some people throw themselves into it, heart and soul, and avatar identity intact. It will be interesting to see whether romances kindled from remote locations create stronger bonds than the ones we were historically able to create in the same room.

It isn't a very high bar to clear.

Pam and I, at least, had a history of spending time in the same air space. We have been together nearly 20 years at this writing, and we have faced many of life's continuing challenges together. We have woven together our families into a set of fulfilling new relationships with (and among) our kids. Her two boys (along with my three kids) have accepted our union, and I am deeply grateful for the opportunity to have a satisfying adult relationship with them. I, for one, could not feel more fortunate for the turn of events that have led us both to a happier marriage than either of us had previously experienced.

I know it is not polite to talk about "getting lucky" with your wife, but I can think of no better way to describe how it is that we find ourselves living, learning, and loving together. But this pool of luck required that both of us act upon the opportunity in order to bring the fruits of our union to bear. People don't always get a second chance for that kind of thing. I feel lucky every day to have been given that second chance (*Proofreaders Note: . . . and so does she*).

The point of all of this mushiness is that Pam and I were lucky to meet each other, but we didn't have the wherewithal to follow-up and pursue our good fortune initially. But thanks to whatever forces were at work, the pathways of our lives were not finished intersecting. The powers-that-be found a way to bring us together again, at a time when we were both lonely and disillusioned. The second time, we were better able to see what we needed and to understand how we could get that from each other. Perhaps, after having been beaten down by life, we were more willing to merge ourselves into the good parts of each other—to commit fully to building a partnership with each other. I can't discount the possibility that the serendipity of our re-connection is truly a blessing from God—and each of us is charged with working hard to realize the power of our opportunity to love one another.

I have no solid evidence to prove whether our reconnection was the work of God, the pull of the planets, or the existence of my lucky silver dollar. But I am thankful for whatever forces were at play. My life would not be as good today without the circumstances (including some significant bad luck in the dissolutions of our previous marriages) that brought us together.

I feel lucky every day that my love life has landed where it has, even though I'm not sure I deserved such good fortune. But how lucky did we all have to be, in the first place, to have come together as a life form on a distant planet on the edge of the Milky Way galaxy? And then to be born in America and be able to put together the pieces of our lives in such a way that someone else would find us to be a desirable partner, warts, scars and all?

So many things have had to come together that it's hard not crediting some of those coincidences to luck. There was a lot more at play than my mere action—responding to an e-mail. That action opened the door to hundreds of other situations, many out of my control, which had to play out in a certain way in order for my love life to have turned out as lucky as it has.

Time spent worrying about the mechanisms of a given situation should not be taken from time you are using to be happy together. I haven't studied what makes Pam and I tick as thoroughly as I should. I'm just grateful that it does.

Identifying key parts of a relationship are important, and help many people, but labeling each of the elements is not as important as simply loving each other. We should start loving others with our instinct, then keep our eyes and our ears open for cues to improve. This helps build empathy and understanding for the prospective partner, and gives you a look at how empathetic they may be in return.

Some of the fellas in high school and college, who understood the mechanisms of physical love, still had a difficult time finding lasting happiness. Lasting happiness requires something more than simply knowing how to pick up a date. We have to understand the terms of the relationship and accept them. We have to develop an earnest ability to see (and appreciate) things from our partner's perspective, even if we don't always see it that way.

In general, treat your significant other the way you'd like to be treated. If we all lived by that one simple rule, the world would be a drastically better place.

I feel blessed, lucky, or in good karma that I have found my balance in love.

REFLECTION QUESTION

How have you been lucky (or unlucky) in love?

Does love require too much work (over the long haul) to allow "luck" a dominant role?

CHAPTER 11

NOW THAT WE'VE FOUND LUCK, WHAT ARE WE GOING TO DO WITH IT?

(apologies to the O'Jays and Third World)

"Some luck lies in not getting what you thought you wanted but getting what you have, which once you have it, you may be smart enough to see is what you would have wanted had you known."

— **Garrison Keillor**, *Lake Wobegon U.S.A.*

We have spent significant ink and paper exploring the origins of luck, which served as the starting point for this writing endeavor. However, at the end of each turn, I have found myself realizing that the origins of luck are not as important as the way in which we react to it.

And luck, all by itself, is scarcely enough to see you through to a satisfying conclusion. You've heard the phrase, "he/she has more luck than sense." Maybe you've even applied it, like I have, to a friend who survived while driving a vehicle at 100 miles per hour down the interstate. Yes, it is an adrenaline rush, but when the road goes past you that fast, you have less time to react to the unforeseeable. Even if you are a good driver, it is a little foolish, but if you are just a weekend hack behind the wheel, driving that fast is really quite stupid. You are opening yourself up to the fates that may exist. Deer jumping across the road, a chunk of ice or asphalt coming to rest in your path, or just another oblivious driver can create the need for diversionary tactics much faster. If you are lucky, you are quick enough to react.

It is the perspective, focus, and common sense we bring into any situation that allows us to access the opportunities for good luck.

As I mentioned early on, had I wallowed in self-pity and drunk myself into oblivion after my unfortunate encounter with the chainsaw, not many people would describe me as lucky. I am lucky because I was able to pursue another direction in which to take my life. I came to an understanding that I had to overcome this facial deformity if my Dad was ever going to forgive himself for his role in the accident.

All I ever had to do was heal my scar, both physically and mentally. Instead of wrestling with guilt and forgiveness, I just had to demonstrate that there was nothing to feel guilty about. There was no forgiveness necessary. I became determined to demonstrate that whatever misfortune came upon my dad and me on that October day in the Colorado mountains, I was going to overcome, have a career, get married, and be okay. All of it really helped to ground my sometimes-wild soul. It gave me a constructive focus in life.

Each of you can also point to a "lucky" development in your life, which is only described as such because you seized the opportunity to make something out of the turn of events.

For those of you who take your luck from the Heavens, it is a common refrain to hear people say, "God doesn't give us challenges bigger than we can handle." We rationalize that there must be a bigger plan that we simply don't understand. I cannot deny the possibility.

Indeed, it is common among the religious community for people to see good and bad developments as nothing more than a test from above to see how we manage our affairs in the context of the Commandments that He has left for us to follow. Those of us blessed with financial wealth should, therefore, be tithing to the church and giving to the poor. Those with physical abilities should reach out to help those who are disabled. Those of us with mental gifts should try to reach out to those with difficulties processing the mental portion of their lives. However, I'm not sure that members of Congress have opened their hearts to receiving any of this kind of help to date.

Those of us to whom bad things have happened, who are also lucky enough to have the wherewithal to carry on as normally as possible, should do so. Especially when that seems to be the best tonic for both ourselves, and for any collateral people consumed by guilt or regret.

If you believe luck is beyond your control, you can blame the position of the planets, or your karma. If you believe your luck is a cause-and-effect relationship to your actions and deeds, then you can commence to blame yourself into a pool of self-loathing. If you believe in superstitions, then any number of circumstances can cause misfortune to result from the prospect of good fortune. Was your lucky coin overpowered by the black cat, which crossed your path?

Whether you believe luck comes from above, from within, from the cosmos, or from your rabbit's foot, it is still up to you to capitalize on your good fortune. There is still a responsibility for each of us to do our part to make good things happen. Sometimes a few turns of good luck really serve as our undoing in a given situation, because we relax, believe our goals will come easily, and lose sight of our responsibility to keep the tide of good fortune rolling.

We have all been born with some innate abilities—and liabilities. For the most part, our portfolio of abilities is similar, but we each have certain things at which we are particularly good (and not so good). Pursuing those things for which we have an instinctive gift helps us to achieve amazing feats. But pursuing things for which our skills are relatively pedestrian can also be rewarding. Sometimes, our success can rise to the level of inspiring others.

For all of the anguish and fighting over the origins of our world, I believe it is our ability to be inspiring—today—to the other humans among us who must advance our species. Inspiring our young people is one of the significant responsibilities distinguishing us from the other animals on this planet.

Or maybe not.

I'm sure, on any trip to any zoo, you could observe other animal species mentoring and inspiring their offspring, in a loving and caring fashion, to excel in the life before them. I can testify from my observations during the last part of the 20th century and the first part of the 21st century, that many human children did not receive timely attention and guidance as they were growing up. It is perhaps a matter of karma that our society gets out of our next generation exactly what it puts into them.

But life is complicated. There are "many rivers to cross," as Jimmy Cliff says. We all must live with the consequences of our decisions. In any decision-making situation, most of us don't dread the decision, itself. We only fear the consequences.

I have been amazed, as I announced to people my intention to quit my job and write a book, how many were sincerely inspired by my actions. Secretly, there must be thousands of people out there who think writing a book would be a marvelous way to make a living (at least it *has* to be better than working at a dead-end job day after day, month after month). Or maybe it is just the inspiration for someone to launch into a project without any guarantee of success that conjures envy up from inside each of us. Call it the American frontiersman spirit, which still simmers inside of a country with scant few frontiers left to explore.

When I reflect, I think it is likely my "previous" self would also be envious of my "current" self, from the outside looking in. I do consider myself lucky to have the opportunity to pursue this writing endeavor. But no matter what happens, there will be consequences. Some good. Some bad.

The pinnacle of my luck is being married to a supportive wife. While I am writing on this project, she is working harder than most people ever dream as an elementary school principal. She comes home most nights completely spent to greet a husband who, at worst, has a sore butt from sitting in an office chair writing his quirky observations all day. Not every wife could tolerate that situation for long. I am lucky she has entertained this project. More than that, she actually played a significant role in hatching the idea of exploring luck during a recent road trip.

What more could a writer ask for than to have a loving, supporting wife who can brainstorm with you, agree to undertake the financial risk of such a dalliance, and even proofread your work along the way?

It's too bad that we sometimes have to take such a scary leap of faith in order to get a "bite at the apple." Yet, every dark cloud in this life does contain a silver lining. That parable is a familiar and recurring theme, as I study the journey of life. Nearly every time, wrapped in a terrible twist of fortune, there is an amazing bit of precious goodness that emerges.

One of my best friends in my previous line of work was Kathy Bartek. Kathy was a school board member from Falls City, Nebraska.

Falls City is a modestly-sized town in the southeast corner of the Cornhusker state.

Kathy, for many years, was the only female member of her school board in Falls City, and worked hard to establish her place in the district's male-dominated decision-making process. She saw the state school boards association as a place of information, enlightenment, and comfort. She liked what she saw enough that she ran for the Board of Directors of the Nebraska Association of School Boards, and eventually became president of the organization. Even after she was president, she helped out by doing facilitation with NASB staff for local boards of education. As I worked alongside her as a consultant for several superintendent searches, we really got to know each other.

It was during this time that I learned, behind all of that public service facade, and a career as a nurse, Kathy was deeply committed to her family.

She was an inspiration to most who knew her, although she was always just a little insecure about her appearance or her presentation. I'm not sure anybody else really ever saw what she was always insecure about. I sure didn't.

For all of the roles that she worked to fulfill, her whole world was suddenly turned upside down in 2011 when Kathy was diagnosed with Lou Gehrig's disease. For those of you who haven't come into contact with Arterial Lateral Sclerosis (the technical name for Lou Gehrig's insidious namesake), this disease is a death sentence. In the nearly eighty years since Gehrig, himself, was reduced from the Ironman of Baseball to a quivering shell of a man, the medical community has failed to make much progress in treating or curing the affliction. It didn't take much research to figure out Kathy had one to three years to live.

As someone who spent her entire professional career in the medical profession, it was clear to her what the diagnosis meant.

After absorbing the shock of such a diagnosis, all of the grandeur and bickering that comes to all of our everyday lives was rendered petty for her. The sometimes-meek woman who didn't want to "act like a big-shot" and often stood back to observe the situation, no longer had time to wait. Everything that she would do, from the point of that diagnosis, was done more purposefully. Everything that came into her view appeared more vividly to her.

There was suddenly nothing too important to keep her from watching her youngest son perform with the University of Nebraska marching band. Spending time with her grandchildren became a precious opportunity—not just for her, but for them. How are they going to remember her ten years from now, or when they become parents and grandparents? Even as the ravages of the disease burrowed away at her ability to write, then walk, then talk, and finally swallow, she reached out for all of the opportunities she could touch.

"Many people who die suddenly of a heart attack or an accident don't get the chance that I have had to say thank you to all of the people who made a difference in their life," Kathy said less than a month prior to her death. "We all have so much to be thankful for. So many people who have helped us along the way. I am very lucky that, with this disease lurking overhead, I no longer miss a chance to thank people."

The poet William Butler Yeats once said, "things reveal themselves passing away." Sometimes we don't realize the preciousness of the people and things in our lives until the precious things approach extinction, or become extinct. That axiom most pointedly applies when we, ourselves, are facing our own mortality. Only some of us are lucky enough to understand that, *and* have the time to express it to those we hold dear.

What Kathy also noted was that, when people opened up and shared with her the contributions she had made, in kind, to their lives, she was able to feel good about her time living among us. What greater gift could any of us receive? While there is no cure for a body ravaged by this disease, Kathy found a powerful cure for her soul—which is living on in the hearts and minds of everyone she touched.

As she raised her family, she often heard her children say, "That's not fair." To which she would reply, "Life isn't supposed to be fair. It's supposed to be worth it." Her impact on the people scattered throughout her life demonstrates to this day that her life was worth it.

None of us has a full appreciation for the ripples our presence on this Earth make in the pool of life. While we all have a finite amount of time on this planet, many of us live our lives as if it's never going to end. As such, we are not as grateful or gracious to those around us. That alone may keep us from realizing all of the luck existing among us every day. So many people contribute to our existence, and make it better than it might have otherwise been, no matter who you are or in what position you find yourself.

There are many people who have blatantly earned our eternal gratitude. There are others, those with the challenging personalities, for whom we should also be thankful. After all, they taught (and continue to teach) us how to endure when things don't go our way. They regularly teach us the value of listening to an opposing viewpoint. They sometimes teach us the power of working together. They sometimes show us how some of our best allies can start as some of our staunchest opponents.

All of these bits of knowledge can be tied up into what we use to maneuver through our lives. While we may initially feel our encounter with a difficult person was unlucky, if we respond appropriately, we can take great value from it. It can turn out to be one of the greatest strokes of good luck to ever happen to us. Perhaps that is why it is important to not let the direction of your life be determined by a single lucky break, good or bad.

It may be too early to determine whether today's result that didn't go our way was fortunate or unfortunate for our long-term existence. Each of us has experienced fate and fortune in our lives, in some scale. We can all look to a time when things did not really roll out the way we had intended, but we persevered.

In the end, Kathy illustrated to me how our luck may be directly tied to our ability to be grateful for all that has befallen us in life. Yes, there have been challenges for everyone. Be grateful that you were able to face those challenges and endure. More importantly, there were many fortunate things that have happened to each of us during our time on Earth. Take the time to recognize the people and circumstances from which our good fortune was launched. If we can simply do that, it isn't hard to recognize just how lucky we all are.

I never became a television anchorman. But television anchorpeople are not really what they used to be anymore. As I watch CNN, and MSNBC, and Fox News, I see so much less news being reported anymore. A majority of their air time is now consumed with opinion, packaged as "analysis," usually from a panel of talking heads who are all eager to interrupt and be heard over the conflicting voices of their fellow panelists. I feel lucky I don't have to referee today's battle of the screaming analysts. There has to be something else I can do that makes more of a meaningful difference.

Today I am able to see, from my current perspective in life, that being tied to a news desk reporting what other people did is not really as rewarding as getting out and doing something myself. In that sense, I should feel very lucky that the chainsaw bounced my way. It kept me out of the middle of what sometimes appears to be the mindless television news business.

Luck, therefore, plays out to be a simple series of events in our life. We get to assign a value to it, whether it is "good" or "bad." But, in the end, it is merely another set of circumstances presented to test our mettle. Can we learn from the experience? Can we accept what has happened and move forward into the next set of circumstances with a positive view of the future? Can we approach the next person who comes into our lives with optimism and a happy disposition? Our own personal answers to these questions can shape how luck will treat us in the future. These are important questions, to which each of us holds our own individual answers.

It is powerful to realize that our luck, regardless of its origins, is shaped by our own perceptions and reactions to it. One person's bad luck could be another's good luck. Something that appears terrible today, may turn out to be the source of your notoriety and success later. Whether you take your cues from the planets, or from God, or from the intricate accounting of karma within your existence, the net result of any given action is ultimately determined by how we respond.

We are all bestowed with abilities and disabilities. Whether you are driven by your disability, like Jim Abbott, or if you are defined by it, is your choice.

It occurs to me, in the course of writing this book, that perhaps luck is merely a mechanism we humans use to generate happiness in our lives, or in some cases sorrow. Perhaps it is merely a human invention to inspire us to hope.

There is so much in this world that seems hopeless and beyond our control. The complications of living in a world with seven billion other souls can be daunting and often overwhelming. We need to find reasons to believe. We need reasons to grasp for hope when things seem to stack up in such a way that we cannot reasonably expect to control the outcome. From our earliest endeavors, life is a series of risks. Learning to walk is one of our earliest experiences. Falling forward, and being able to catch ourselves with our next step takes a little practice. Repeating that over and over again until we can walk, and then run, starts a perpetual cycle of risks and rewards which, stacked end to end, create the story of our lives.

In order to take that first step, we need to be encouraged that we *can* be successful. We need hope in order to bolster our faith that we can advance from a stumbling toddler into a mobile adult. Once we master one challenge, life is all about looking for the next possibility, developed from (and dependent upon) a new set of hopes.

All we have in this world, beyond our own humble abilities, is the hope that we can endure. If we succeed, all the better. But we fundamentally need to endure until we find the right opportunity into which we can successfully fit.

That is why I find it difficult to disparage any of the tools of luck discussed in this book. If you can nurture your spirit by finding something that works for you and, as long as it doesn't deprive people of life, liberty, or the pursuit of happiness (sacrificing virgins or inflicting death or serious harm on another human is just not proper as a springboard for your luck), I think you ought to go for it. You owe it to yourself, your creator, and everyone else who may benefit from the alignment of circumstances allowing you to move forward.

Who am I to define *for you* what is lucky or unlucky? If your brand of luck works for you, I hope you can enjoy it regularly.

If your pursuit of luck leads you to eating healthier and living a healthier lifestyle, who could it really hurt?

Perhaps there truly is an undercurrent in our consciousness urging us to make the right choice, or helping us to always land on our feet. If you can get that channel through your Bluetooth, rock on!

Or perhaps you believe our entire existence on Earth—every detail— is dictated and decided by your Divine Creator. Your own personal deliverance is your own business, which means my deliverance is *my* business. While I bristle a little at the weak spots within organized religion, I believe there is a Divine Creator. And if you do too, God bless you. If you don't, may you find good luck on your path, too.

Many people, throughout human existence, have tried to promote various tonics, religions, and dances to bring about the best possible results. Many more will continue. It is up to you to decide what works for you.

With personal decisions as monumental as success or failure, we should be motivated to take an active role in determining what gives our situation the most hope and the best chance for success. Nobody else is as interested in your success as you are.

Maybe our method of luck simply lights a fire in our bellies to help us more urgently pursue our goals.

Maybe a little luck adds momentum to the strategic vision after we experience the beginning of a "plan coming together."

Even simple things can start the ball rolling. Don't we all get an extra lilt in our step when we find plenty of time on the parking meter we just pulled up to? Don't we all look at the world just a little differently when we find a penny (face-up, of course) on the ground with no apparent owner?

None of these things are significant financial windfalls, but they present us with the invaluable opportunity to take them as a sign that something positive is within our grasp. Maybe the winds of fortune will blow our way at the next appointment. Maybe our biorhythms are lining up and this is our day of destiny. Time to straighten the tie and put the best foot forward to greet this opportunity. Which, of course, increases the odds that you will be successful. Good luck begets more good luck.

On the other hand, how many of us have stubbornly pursued our goals with the philosophy that "the system owes me" even after we have been initially turned away. After all, if nine out of ten attempts fail, and I've tried nine times unsuccessfully, I'm due to break through. This is an approach I've embraced during the ordeal of writing, publishing and distributing this book. I'm sure each of you can cite your own examples of perseverance winning the day, eventually. In many cases, the spoils go to the stubborn. Those unwilling to quit are, by sheer force of will, more likely to see their dreams through to fruition.

Thomas Edison, one of the greatest minds in American history once said, "Many of life's failures are people who did not realize how close they were to success when they gave up."

You, no doubt, have come into contact with people who have mastered the art of creating a defeatist attitude based on their circumstances, where a couple of unfavorable turns leave them wanting nothing more than to quit. If that attitude is allowed to grow, it becomes impossible to pursue our dreams. That's worse than unlucky.

I have referred previously to the axiom, "what you focus on in life will grow." Focus on the shreds of good luck in your life, and you can create a beautiful quilt. Focus on the bad luck, and you will wallow in a pile of scrap.

This is not to say that you should base your entire life on whether luck enters into your physical space today, or tomorrow. Great success depends on careful planning, with liberal measures of skill and experience working into the mix. If you sit in your chair and wait for luck to deliver you fame and fortune, your chances of attaining your goals are infinitesimally small. You have to analyze any given situation, consider the options that will deliver you to the plan, and take action to see your vision through to reality.

Along the way, some things will work as you visualized them, and some things will not. In each of those situations, luck may certainly be a factor. But luck alone cannot win (or lose) the day. Luck happens every once in a while, but we cannot depend on luck to build the boat and sail us to a distant shore. We still must do our share of the work to realize our dreams, no matter what happens along the way.

The complicated part of this is that, sometimes, the stars are lined up for our success, and it is our contributions that keep it from happening. Therefore, it is important to constantly reflect on the progress you are making toward your goals, not only to analyze where things are going right and wrong, but to also make sure you are not an impediment to the plan's success.

All that being said, it is hard to ignore that each of us have already overcome long odds by having our ions land on the only planet in this solar system to support our kind of life. We again fulfilled the chemical probability that we could be born in the human form. We also overcame obstacles to obtain an education and learn to read (or to be born into a society where audio books will read this to you). Living well has proven for most of us an even higher level of challenge. Being successful in this life (even though *you* get to define your own success) can provide the longest of odds.

Just being here on Earth in the 21st century is a miracle of incredible magnitude. All of the other obstacles on our path to success are merely created by humans. Things created by humans can be overcome by humans. Nothing about living in this world comes easy, but we each have the power to overcome. If a few heartening signs of good fortune can illuminate our paths, I see that as a good thing. I don't have to believe what you believe in. If it works for you, congratulations.

Mitch Albom, in his book "Have a Little Faith: A True Story," says, "The secret to happiness...be satisfied and be grateful." I believe if finding a penny on the ground, or carrying a rabbit's foot in your pocket, helps you accomplish those keys to happiness, nobody should throw cold water on them.

Every major accomplishment depends on many minor things to go right. A positive feeling which energizes us to push forward toward our ultimate goal is one of those things that needs to go right. Malcolm Gladwell confirms this in his book, "The Outliers." His analogy relates to airline disasters, where the cause of nearly every modern commercial plane crash has proven to have multiple sources. The same is true with incredibly positive outcomes. We can't have a major positive development in our lives without several smaller situations turning our way, often without our knowledge or influence.

As we have discovered, the determining factor in whether we have good luck or bad in the future is, how are we going to respond to today's developments? Can we "tuck and roll," and keep moving forward? No other source of luck is nearly as pivotal as the power we each possess to define our own destinies.

Throughout this book, we are driven back to one ultimate truth about luck. Its very existence, and indeed its impact, is in the eyes of the beholder. We have the power to define the luck in our lives. Therefore, the rest of the work in defining your luck is up to you. Take a long look at your life and your soul and do an honest assessment.

Are you lucky?

"SO, WHAT DO YOU KNOW?"

ABOUT THE AUTHOR.

Well, it's a valid question.

A lot of people have asked me that question, in one form or another, while I have interviewed for a variety of jobs throughout my life. So it is in all ways fitting that my readers should wonder the same thing.

In fact, it is a question that lurks in every author's lack of self-confidence—including mine. Why should anyone care about my opinions of luck?

I certainly don't profess to be an expert on the subject. But I have had experiences during my life that have caused me to visit fate's doorstep. The turning of the millennium has been a wonderful time to live in the center of the United States of America. The last half of the 20th century brought with it a blossoming of culture and self-exploration. The first few years of the 21st century have been consumed with the consequences of a culture which has over-indulged itself in its self-exploration. My self-indulgent generation of the 1960s, 70s and 80s has now given birth to a new generation who is not tethered to any particular code of conduct. Many of them raised themselves.

If we are to have any hope of gluing together the pieces of our shattered society, it must start with an honest self-reflection of who we are and how we can be better in the future.

Although this book is something less than a scholarly work, some of the items contained in this book are footnoted in order to provide you with additional deeper reading in the areas from which I was reporting.

Other observations are a synthesis of several people (who are often alluded to), who have all asserted something similar, but really never put it in these exact words. In no cases, do I ever hope to be as smart (or as competent) as any of the people I have drawn from in their given fields. Still, their words and findings are valuable as we attempt to find a path for our personal belief system.

Still other comments throughout the book, while they were certainly influenced by the stories that have come before my eyes, are strictly from the archives of my own observations in watching and working with people.

I have earned a Bachelor's Degree (Journalism) from the University of Northern Colorado, and a Master's Degree (Educational Administration) from the University of Nebraska at Lincoln. I can heartily assure you that in both cases (which were quite different experiences, at quite different times in my life), I learned infinitely more from watching and listening to people than I did from the pages of my overpriced textbooks. Many of the things I have learned in life were from people who never darkened the doorway of a university classroom. Of course, I did emblazon onto my mind certain facts from Walter Stewart's 8 a.m. Journalism History class that allowed me to pass the test. "Acursy, Acursy, Acursy," he used to say, with an accent that made it so ironic—and unforgettable. Accuracy remains the most important element of my writing, even if it is regularly ignored by others in much higher positions of the media. It also turned out that I learned an awful lot about myself along the way, particularly how I might react to others when they act unpredictably around me.

To this day, studying human behavior and interaction is what consumes most of my time—whether I am in traffic, in the grocery store, or just reading the paper. People are certainly interesting creatures. Individually, they are among the smartest animals on the planet. But when you put them into a group, things can quickly turn into another impromptu episode of "I Love Lucy."

So much of what we humans do, as a collective, is destructive and hurtful. Talking about the positive aspects, such as luck, doesn't get as much exposure. I was surprised at how little the concept of luck has been studied—or written about—in the past.

Yet, rarely does a month go by when we do not see a couple of stories about a lucky lottery winner or a miracle survivor of a natural or manmade disaster. Almost weekly in sports, we see a fluke bounce, or a bad officiating call, make the difference between victory and defeat.

As we have seen time and again, people will always be looking for ways to create a "system" through which to manage (or get an upper hand on) fate. For many, this means preparation for an array of situations in an effort to render luck impotent. But even when you get to the end of what you prepared for, there is the element of fate.

Both sides have prepared well, which way will the ball (or the grenade) bounce?

It has occurred to me that perhaps studying the characteristics of luck was in itself unlucky, thus deterring any would-be academicians from further study. But then it occurred to me, if anyone was listing their profession as academician, perhaps luck has already cast the heaviest of burdens upon them. What more do they have to fear?

There is a tremendous amount of academic ground to be covered on this subject, and I commend the research frontier to those eager to uncover answers for some of the many questions for which mankind has not yet determined a "right" or a "wrong" solution. For all of their flaws, humanity is innately inquisitive. That gives me confidence that people will continue to explore the frontiers of what we know on the subject of luck, positivity, and human behavior. Hopefully this exploration and debate will happen with a minimal amount of bloodshed.

As for this book, I hope you will judge it from the perspective in which it was written. As a trained journalist, I appreciate the value of a good story. Compelling stories of real people is what I went in search of as I wrote this book. Everything described in these stories is true.

I have done my best to make sure that specific things attributed to specific people are specifically correct. I have made sustained efforts to establish personal contact with anyone whose story has been told in this book. That doesn't mean that their story (or its depiction herein) is the final word. There are untold numbers of people who have served in the military, been involved in a serious accident or illness, or pitched in the major leagues, or have thrown their luck to the wind as gamblers, who have unique—and quite likely—more amazing stories of luck than these. Other people might have been sitting right next to the people I talked to at the moment the pivotal event occurred—and as such, had a slightly different perspective. I just didn't interview them.

I am so grateful for the vast array of experiences in my life, but I am most truly humbled by the opportunity to watch (and help) others as we all try to advance to the "next stage" of life, whatever that may be.

Luck be with you!

www.ingramcontent.com/pod-product-compliance
Lightning Source LLC
Chambersburg PA
CBHW060800120626
46557CB00001B/46